BUTTING HEADS IN SPAIN

Lady Goatherder 1

DIANE ELLIOTT

Ant Press

MAP SHOWING LAS VICARIAS AND SURROUNDS

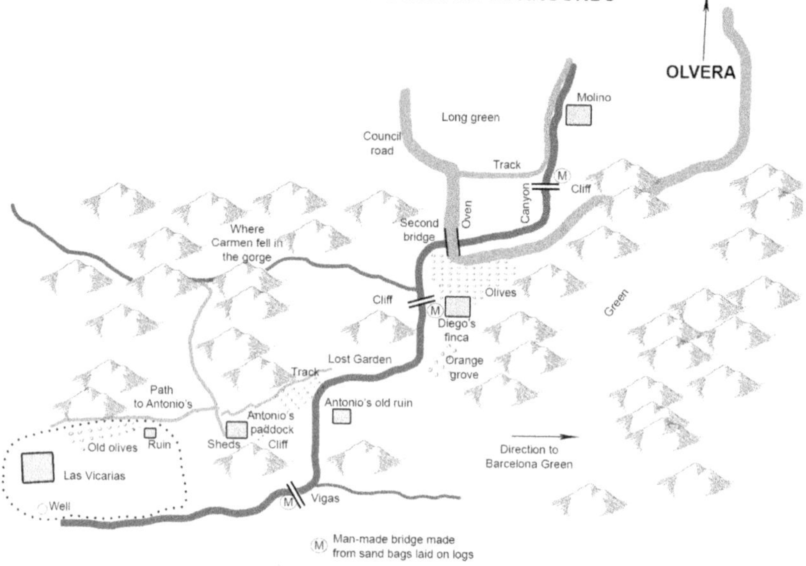

See this map and photos at
https://antpress.org/lady-goatherder-gallery/

Cover painting of Alice by Mikki Rowland

Formatted and published by Ant Press, 2022

Paperback Edition ISBN: 978-1-922476-56-2

Hardback Edition ISBN: 978-1-922476-57-9

Large Print Edition ISBN: 978-1-922476-58-6

Large Print Hardback Edition ISBN: 978-1-922476-59-3

Photographs property of Diane Elliott

Praise for Diane Elliott

"Gripping, fun and full of animal magic. This quirky memoir will charm you." Beth Haslam, author of the Fat Dogs and French Estates series.

"Orange-munching goats and dogs who speak with a Prince Charles accent, I loved this book." Elizabeth Moore, author of the Someday Travels series and Top 1000 Amazon reviewer.

"What a gorgeous book. I laughed and (happy) cried from start to finish." Victoria Twead, New York Times bestselling author of the Old Fools series.

"A joy, a delightful mix of tense and tender moments." Julie Haigh, Goodreads Librarian and Top 500 Amazon reviewer.

Dedicated to Eileen

Eileen Grace Hair
25th November 1960 - 25th January 2016

Contents

1

Lady Goatherder

"Alice, get out of that olive tree, we're ready to go. I can see you behind that branch."

She doesn't even flinch. I turn to another olive tree and my voice goes up a notch.

"Willow, I'm warning you. Get down now."

Mother and daughter ignore me. Time to call my husband.

"Pete, grab an orange from the Alice Bucket and a large stone."

The Alice Bucket is a store of sour oranges we collect from our single orange tree. It hangs on a hook in the paddock, ready for emergencies like this. Peter hobbles in and returns, fruit in one hand, large stone in the other. His six-foot frame is stooped, due to heaving a sack of pony nuts from the car to the feed store two days ago. Backache makes him walk like a duck with a wooden leg.

Peter is an excellent shot. Handing me the little orange bribe, he takes aim, hits the olive tree and Willow leaps out with that familiar teenage look, mouthing the word, *whatever*. Alice smells the orange, slowly climbs back down to terra firma, snatches the offered fruit from my hand and devours it in one chew. Willow and Alice rejoin the others who are patiently waiting in the big field.

"Are we ready, girls?" I ask my thirty friends.

Chinita, or Chinni, watches me, waiting for the command. This lady's life has been plagued with ill health and an old illness has returned. This may be her last long walk. She knows it but is determined to make this day her finest.

Chinni is the head of my herd of goats. Tall and graceful with large horns that curl neatly behind her ears. Her brown and white speckled colouring, and splash of white blaze, makes her stand out amongst the rest of the girls. Well, that and her IQ.

My fellow goat herder, and neighbour, Antonio, with over 30 years of experience working with goats, told me that she was one in a billion. He, as always, is right.

Antonio's two hundred goats are waiting for me on the other side of the river, up an embankment, where most are sleeping under the eucalyptus trees.

"Hello girls!" I shout to them. "We'll be off in a jiffy."

No reply. I'd have thought that by now they would have picked up a smidgen of English, but obviously not. I leap from stone to stone across the river, showing great enthusiasm. My girls, led by Chinni, follow me.

We join Antonio's goats. All two hundred and thirty goats will be crossing and re-crossing the river as we make our way upstream.

The phone rings. It's Antonio.

"Have you got enough water?"

"Yes."

"Food?"

"Yes."

"Oranges?"

"Yes, yes, yes."

"Okay, I'm sending the dogs down the track to you. Good luck."

My neighbour, friend, and teacher in all things goat, decided that I should take his two hundred girls across country to their summer residence.

His main residence, at the end of the track linking our properties, becomes unbearably hot in the summer. So he moves upriver to the family owned Mill, the *Molino*. With large eucalyptus trees surrounding the old building, his goats can relax and be shaded from the sun in the intense summer heat.

It is difficult for him to hand over his precious herd to the Englishwoman, especially as his reputation of not damaging other peoples' olive trees is at stake. Allowing me to walk the herd will free him to transport all the feed troughs, chickens, and assorted equipment in his tractor and trailer. Normally, Peter would help him move, but lifting that sack of horse food has put him out of action.

This will also be his student's 'end of school' exam. My chance to show that a middle-aged English woman can handle over two hundred goats alone. It could also be madness.

I adjust my cowboy-style straw hat and shoulder my water carrier. I'm ready. The phone rings again.

"Change of plan. The dogs won't leave and have jumped into the tractor."

"What?"

"And the two old girls have escaped and are heading your way."

"What?"

"Look, leave them at the lost garden, if they get that far, and I will pick them up later in the Land Rover."

"WHAT!"

"Oh, and five babies have climbed out of the trailer and are running fast down the track to you. Don't worry, they will find their mums. Just watch them when you reach the cliffs."

The phone goes dead but I keep yelling into it for another twenty seconds. So now I have no dogs. It is too late to go back for my two working dogs. Anyway, they've probably got the hump because I'd left them behind.

There are seven olive groves to pass and in the herd I have two old girls, Sniffy and the Abuela (grandmother). Sniffy is disabled and the Abuela is suffering from dementia. It is also forty degrees.

I tell myself it's all just a minor setback.

"Come on ladies, let's go, hup, hup, hup!"

My thirty goats slowly start to rise, but Antonio's mob continue to sit and talk amongst themselves. The two old girls finally stumble down the steep slope to the river and promptly collapse in the sand.

"It's time to move girls. Hup, hup!"

I begin to feel like a supply teacher addressing Class 5C.

Thankfully, Chinni takes over. Turning to the herd she flicks her head and turns back to me, her eyes meeting mine. All of Antonio's goats stand and start to walk towards me.

How did she do that?

"Good girl Chin. Let's cross the river."

The first river crossing is an easy one. Stones stretch from one side of the bank to the other. The river is clear, warm and calf-deep. I find this out by slipping off the first stone. I turn around to see who has noticed. Antonio's two hundred goats snigger. No matter. In this heat my boots will be dry in twenty minutes. Or less.

Chinni sets the pace and the goats follow closely behind. I guard the olive trees, running backwards and forwards, waving my stick at anyone who glances at the inviting saplings. The sun beats down. I have drunk nearly one litre of water and we are only half an hour into the journey.

"Wait, Chinni," I call, motioning with my hand for her to slow down.

As she halts, two hundred and thirty goats dive into the shade of tall cane grass that grows along the river banks. It is 12:30 pm and the heat is on.

Sniffy and the Abuela catch up, walking as if they are holding on to Zimmer frames.

"Okay everyone," I say to the already sleeping goats, "take five."

Goats were not on our 'when we move to Spain' list. Pony trekking was. Horses had always been my life and the dream to work with them every day was one that I had put on hold for years. Life, marriage, children and work, all came first. But I had a dream. Moving to Spain would, at last, make it come true.

Luckily for me Peter also shared my dream. Before we married, in 1999, I had told him that, eventually, I wanted to move to Andalucia.

"That'd be bostin'. Can we goo now?" he had said in his broad Birmingham accent.

Mentally I translated that to mean, jolly good, I'm on board. His accent was lost many years ago and only surfaces when he is talking to his family or when he is drunk. But he enjoys watching me, a Kentish lass, struggle with the finer points of a West Midlands accent.

Our dream remained on hold for many years. Peter was working in our local theatre, as a lighting and sound technician, in a small coastal town in Dorset. I took on summer cleaning jobs in order to be home for the children. We have four between us, with two living at home.

After my father died, mum's health had gone rapidly downhill. My sister became her main home carer and every two weeks I travelled up to Kent to give Sandra a break.

Pete and I juggled work and home life. The dream of Spain was somewhere in the future, but we kept the dream alive. We planned the move with another couple, who also wanted to change their lives.

My youngest daughter, Felicity (Fliss) and I have two gorgeous cob horses. Beau, black and white, 14.2 hands high (hh), is a real charmer. Apart from his beauty, his Dublin heredity has seduced humans and mares alike. Hardy, my big boy, had reached 16.1 hh, a bay with a white blaze. Handsome, yes, but lacking Beau's style.

He reminds me of the Colonel in the television comedy, *Fawlty Towers*. Most of his vocabulary consists of, "What ho, old bean! Tally ho!" and "Well done, old chap!" Although we owned two acres of land, situated next to a nature reserve, there were few bridleways close by. In summer months, Fliss and I got up at silly o'clock to ride across the town to the hills and forestry.

The riding was wonderful and some years we were able to rent land for a few months and enjoy riding every day. The winter months were awful. Our land was flooded in one corner and the lower part of the land became a muddy swamp.

After years of winter rains, we became used to our Wellington boots being sucked down into the mud, leaving us no option but to continue to the field shelter in socks. I used to giggle at the sight of my socks turning into flippers.

I giggled as I walked from my car to the house, holding dripping socks and mud-clogged Wellington boots. Then one evening I stopped giggling and cried. I'd had enough. Maybe it was time to really start planning our escape to a warmer climate. Four years later, we realised our dream.

We had spent the last four years planning and searching for the ideal property. We needed a house that was big enough to be split into two dwellings, one for each family, outbuildings to be converted into two holiday cottages, and land for the horses.

Las Vicarias fitted the bill. Not only did it have two houses and assorted outbuildings, it also had seven acres of flat land, ideal for a horse-schooling ring, and paddocks. With ninety olive trees, an old ruin and the River Guadalporcun gently flowing at the bottom of the land, it was heaven.

Both sets of families had aging parents. Being together ensured we had a good support system should one couple need to dash back to England.

I managed to sell my cottage and land in a day. Our friends took a little longer. Eventually we were ready to pack and wave goodbye to one life and start a new adventure.

My two old cats, Jake and Tilly, cost us a fortune to prepare them for the plane journey over. They needed to have their teeth checked and a general overhaul. The horses had never been boxed before but the horse-transporters reassured me that they would be fine. I worried.

Our move over was simple. Our belongings were mainly boxes and boxes of books, horse tack and Pete's guitars. Everything else I sold or gave away. The other couple had a few more items as their furniture was in far better shape than ours. We loaded the transport lorry and flew out the next day.

The cats seemed none the worse for their flight. They immediately settled in at the farm, enjoying the warm air and the freedom to climb olive trees and sunbathe in the shade of the pomegranate trees. The horses arrived eight days later. We met the lorry at the top of our track and before the ramp could be lowered I called out to them.

I heard a deep whicker. The doors opened and there were my boys. We walked them slowly back to the farm and let them out into the newly fenced field. They drank and then both had the longest pee I have ever witnessed.

Their four day journey to Las Vicarias seemed not to have fazed them at all. My worries were for nothing. They were enjoying a new adventure. Both rolled and then got their heads down to munch. The humans opened a bottle of wine. We did it. All was well, or so we thought.

Six weeks later, the other couple found that *campo* (countryside) life was not for them after all, and left. We were in deep shock at first and then realised that we had to buy them out. That left us with no money to renovate the houses, connect to electricity, or start up a business.

For us, there was no going back. I had sold my house and land, the two horses were here and both cats were enjoying the Spanish heat. We had to do something. But what? Antonio stepped in.

As with most Spaniards who find themselves with English neighbours, they feel obliged to take over the *extranjeros* (foreigners') lives. Antonio, although a rather solitary man, took over as soon as we moved in. Blonde-haired, blue-eyed, ten years younger than us, he was an obsessive animal person. It had been rumoured that his great grandfather was English but nobody in his family talked about it.

He organised the building of stables, trimmed trees, lopping off branches with a chain saw in one hand and a cigarette in the other. He was not bothered about the language barrier.

"I can talk dog, goat, horse and mule. So I'm sure I can manage to talk to you English."

Had he been lucky enough to have had a good education, he wanted to be a physiotherapist. As it was he left school at fourteen to work on the land. By the time he was twenty five he had a tractor and was dividing his time between contract work on farms and construction. At the same time he was slowly building up a goat herd. His days started at 5 am and finished at around 11 pm.

I should have been suspicious, one evening, when he invited himself down to the farm for a hot chocolate.

"Goats are the answer," he announced.

"No. But thank you for the suggestion," I said, looking over at Pete for support.

"You have two youngsters already and I'll start you off with another two."

Evidently he hadn't heard a word I said.

"We don't know anything about a dairy herd," I said, "it's not a good idea."

I openly stared at my silent husband to jump in.

"He's taking over again," I mouthed to Pete. "Help, for goodness sake."

"We could buy you thirty fully grown goats," Antonio continued, "but you'd kill them off. Goat school starts tomorrow when you bring the kids up for milk."

Leaving us to digest his words, he stubbed out his cigarette and left.

"Why didn't you back me up?" I demanded, turning furiously to Pete.

"Well, maybe it's a good idea. I mean, think about it. Two English people become goat herders. What an adventure!"

He took another sip of beer.

"Are you drunk or just bloody insane?" I spat.

"Probably both, Di. But I think we should at least give it a try. What have we got to lose? Antonio is right, we already have two girls and we have to start somewhere."

I took myself outside and sat with the horses to think. I couldn't believe that Peter had fallen for this crazy idea of Antonio's. I wanted to shout and stamp my foot but in truth, I couldn't blame him for clutching onto a way out of our predicament.

Who could I blame then? Oh wait, I know. Bloody Rafael! Yep, he is to blame for all of it!

Rafael, the soon-to-be-retired goat herder from a farm way downriver, had given us two baby goats.

"A gift for you English," he announced, as he chucked the little things out of his car.

Peter and I stared at the kids as they struggled to get to their feet. I met Peter's eyes. We both knew that to turn down these gifts would be insulting to our new neighbour. Practicality quickly set in.

"How do I feed them, Rafael?"

"Take them to Antonio's and he will sort them out."

He left us staring at the sweet bundles. I called Antonio.

"I'll come down," he said.

Antonio loves babies, and he loves to name them.

"This one," he said, as he held the little ebony girl high in the air, "this one we will call Pepita."

Peter gave me the now familiar 'he is taking over again' look.

"And this one," Antonio said, holding the speckled brown one aloft. "This one we will call Alicia."

"Alicia? Why?"

"I don't know. Names just come to me."

The next day Rafael turned up with a pretty white lamb.

"Now you have a sheep. They are much better than goats."

"Antonio is not naming the bloody sheep. I am!" Peter cuddled the white lamb tightly to his chest. "I name her Carmen."

As cute as they were, I didn't want any more animals dumped on us. We needed time to think and plan. No added responsibilities. That all changed after Antonio's visit.

At 8:30 the following morning, I walked up the steep track to Antonio's sheds, carrying Pepita and Alicia, Carmen trotting behind me. After feeding my girls on any one of Antonio's goats that had spare milk, I popped them into a pen. I grabbed a beer crate, ready to sit and learn how to hand milk. My teacher just stared at me.

"Any idiot can milk a goat. Keeping them alive is what you need to learn."

He ushered me up to the first line of tied goats that were waiting to be milked.

"Feel every teat and see if you can detect any heat."

He turned his back and continued to hand-milk his girls, none of whom were impressed with the English woman's feeble attempts to grope their udders. They kicked, sat down, and waved horns in my general direction.

I couldn't find any difference in heat in any of the hundred-odd goats I groped. Sadly for them, this lesson went on for seven days. Then I had a breakthrough.

"I can feel something different," I said.

I felt triumphant, but the broad grin was soon wiped off my face.

"About time, I have been treating that goat for two days now."

Grabbing my hand he shoved it under the goat's teat.

"As I squirt the milk, feel the difference in texture."

He squirted and I looked blank.

He then squirted from her good side.

"Let the milk run through your fingers."

Okay so far. Then he squirted her bad side onto my hand.

"Now can you feel the difference?"

I did. Then I asked him what drugs she needed. The medicine cabinet was opened and he explained what drugs to administer, why, how much and how often.

Day after day I walked up the track with the babies following me. It was always the same routine. Enter the shed, remove coat, hands on teats. By the end of the month I could guess a goat's weight, administer drugs and spot a tick on an ear at fifty paces. Antonio donated two more babies. Ruby and Lucy joined our herd.

It was close to birthing time at Antonio's. He would phone if he needed any help in the evenings. It had been a long, cold day. We had been collecting wood and organising the house on the promise of rains to come. In short, it meant collecting buckets and placing them upstairs at potential leak-sites under the roof.

The phone call came at 10 pm.

"Little Ronnie has some problems, get up here."

Grabbing coats and torches, we scuttled up the track. I visualised delivering my first baby, a new life and new beginnings. Antonio had promised to give me Ronnie's first born. We entered the dimly lit shed to find Ronnie tied up to the large feed trough, groaning.

"Wash your hands, go in and get the baby out," he said. "She has stopped pushing and my hands are too big to manoeuvre it."

My idea of helping deliver a baby was to catch the little thing before it hit the ground, clean it up and offer it to the mum. I stared at the rear end of little Ronnie, then stared at Peter. He gave me a sympathetic sort of smile.

"What are you waiting for? The goat is in trouble Diane," Antonio said, completely unaware of my horror.

"What do I do?" I tried to sound confident.

"Gently feel your way in first."

I took a deep breath and went in. All I could feel was mush.

"I can't feel anything except goo!"

This was relayed to Antonio in English. He understood. He knew perfectly well what I was touching, despite my limited Spanish. He lifted her tummy up.

"Now feel."

I touched two thin legs. Relaying this information in English, Antonio told me, in Spanish, that the baby was dead and to grab the legs and lift my index finger up to feel for the head.

Again I just felt mush but then, "Bingo!" I touched a hard mass.

"Pull," he said.

"I'll pull the legs off. They're too thin."

"Get it out or Ronnie will die." A cold stare met mine.

I steadily pulled the two twigs and, with my other finger, kept the head down.

"It will smell a bit," he said, his nose already starting to wrinkle.

Taking a deep breath, I finally pulled the little creature out. Antonio went to work on Ronnie, washing her and giving her some antibiotics. Pete and I stared at the undeveloped baby. It dawned on me that Antonio didn't really need my help to extract this dead baby. This was a test.

"Well done, Lady Dee," said Antonio using the new nickname he had bestowed on me.

The next day I was called upon to deliver again.

"This should be an easy one. Just go in and feel that the position is good," he said, spitting out his umpteenth roll-up.

"I can feel three legs, and one is on top of the head."

For some reason I started to blink rapidly. It must have been a nervous reaction.

"Move," he said, pushing me out of the way. "Shit, shit! We have two babies all tangled up."

It took twenty minutes of pushing, pulling, and swearing before he finally extracted two big boys. He saw my eyes blinking. I just couldn't stop them.

"Don't worry," he said, patting my shoulder. "It's not always this bad."

He was right of course. Over the following three weeks I delivered baby after baby. I delivered on the sides of hills and in deep gorges. I often carried four babies over my shoulders, their front legs tied up with string, their mums bumping into me, checking that I was not murdering their new offspring.

If I could just master eating a sardine with a penknife, then I'd have this *campo* life sorted!

Ruby and Lucy, Antonio's gifts, moved into Las Vicarias. Pepita and Alice had more playmates. Carmen, although happy to sleep and eat with the young goats, didn't want to play with them. She watched as the four youngsters played. They jumped on and off rocks and ran up and down the hill behind the house. Carmen never once joined in. I worried.

"Do you think there is something wrong with her?" I asked Pete. "She just follows me around."

"There's nothing wrong with Carmen. She just can't see the point in running around in the heat, that's all. She's an intelligent girl." Peter sounded very confident in his diagnosis.

Coming back from the town one morning, we passed Rafael on the track.

"I've left a little present for you English," he shouted out of his car window.

"What sort of present?"

"A pretty little kid. You will love her. But she's sick and will probably die tonight." He drove off before we could utter another word.

Sure enough, curled up in a cardboard box outside our door was the most beautiful tiny baby. I picked her up and cuddled her. She was very floppy and very thin. Antonio had just arrived back at the sheds. I phoned.

"Rafael has done it again, Antonio, and this baby is sick. Can you help?"

"Bring her up, let me look at her."

He gently examined the little girl.

"She has pneumonia and she is not looking good. Underweight too, probably hasn't eaten in days."

"Can we save her?"

"I don't know, Diane, but I will try. First, I need to get some colostrum into her. Just a bit, not too much. Then, some antibiotics. We have a fight on our hands to keep this little one alive so don't build your hopes up."

"We have to try. She is so pretty." I held her tight to me.

"She looks like a little china doll," said Antonio. "I name her Chinita."

We bottle fed her around the clock, little and often, and Antonio gave her a course of antibiotics. She slept by the side of our bed, sometimes inside it, and slowly she began to respond.

I made the decision to move her into the stable with the other goats and Pete made a little pen for her, filling it with straw. Her last bottle was now at midnight. At 5:30 the next morning we crept into the stable, warm milk bottle in hand. Chinita was up, ready for her breakfast. Carmen had slept next to her pen all night.

While the four youngsters played on the hillside, Chinni, Carmen and I pottered around the olive grove. Carmen was now Chinita's governess and protector. As the weeks passed by, Chinni wanted to join the goats as they ran for the hill and bounced on the boulders. Carmen clearly didn't think Chin was strong enough. One 'baaa!' and a firm stare was enough to make Chinni run back to her side.

Another week went by until it finally happened. I opened the gate for the girls to play and Carmen led Chinni up the hill to join the family. She kept watch as Chin jumped from rock to rock, following her big sisters. After half an hour, Carmen led Chinni back down again.

Antonio had said it was time the youngsters walked with the big herd, telling me to bring Chinni out as well, and to stop mollycoddling her. I wondered if Carmen would allow it.

"Who is in charge of your goats, you or Carmen?" said Antonio.

"Carmen, I think. I will talk to her tonight and see if she feels Chinni is ready."

Antonio stared at me, not sure if I was joking or not. I wasn't.

The following afternoon, I opened the paddock gate and looked at Carmen before turning and starting to walk up the track towards Antonio's. The four girls followed me, bouncing madly. Carmen had made her decision and Chinita flipped her head with joy.

Chinni leading the herd.

2

The River

It's time to move on. I grab my water bottle and walking stick. Chinni is already up and waiting, her eyes scanning the herd.

"Okay ladies, let's go!"

My voice startles them. Instead of moving off sedately, they dash in different directions, some scrabbling up the steep banks by the river, others making a run into the precious olive groves.

"Chinni, do something!" I yell, throwing a stone in the general direction of a goat munching on an olive branch.

Chinni turns and walks towards the track leading to the 'lost garden'. She ducks under the brambles and is out of sight to me and the goats. Thankfully, my girls dash after her.

Antonio's mob, not wanting to be left behind with the shouting English woman, trot after them. Abuela and Sniffy look confused as goats scuttle past them. Determined not to be left behind, they grab their Zimmer frames and begin their slow shuffle to catch up.

Chinni keeps the goats at a steady pace and I run up and down alongside them, keeping them away from the olive groves. The cicadas are in full voice, the males impressing the females with their deafening sound. They vibrate membranes in their abdomen which proves the saying that the way to a man's heart is through his stomach.

One more turn and we'll be at the lost garden. It's so named because the deeds to this piece of land were lost many years ago. Rumour has it, however, that a chap called 'The Moro' owns it... sort of.

It is a flat piece of land with an old ruin on it. At the edge of the river bank are many eucalyptus trees that provide perfect shade. We come here during birthing time. If five or more give birth, Antonio brings the Land Rover down to pick up the mums and babies. It's here that I will leave Antonio's two old girls for him to collect later. The long walk to the garden will have completely tired them out.

As the last goat turns the corner, I look back to check on Antonio's pensioners. All I can see is two bobbing dots in the distance. Not to worry, they'll get to us in their own time. I walk around the bend and bump into Chinni who is waiting for me.

Together we walk to the herd. The girls are making themselves at home, drinking in the river and eyeing up the best sleeping spots. I climb down the bank and take off my boots and socks. It is pure bliss sinking my hot, sweaty feet into the cool water.

With my cheese sandwiches on my lap, I listen to the river gently bubbling over the rocks. I close my eyes. The water running over my throbbing feet starts to lull my fried brain into a sleepy stupor. Yes, pure bliss. Then the memory of the Christmas of 2009 comes flooding back.

I promised our beautiful old house in Spain that we would repair it as soon as my long-lost, mega-rich uncle turned up. Meanwhile we had to sort out immediate difficulties. We needed a shower, a loo, and a kitchen. Time, money, and lack of building knowledge held us up. What we really needed was advice and a miracle.

Pete and I had arrived at the local bar and ordered coffee. Sitting outside, we tackled the paperwork, sent to us by the *Junta de Andalucia* (local authorities), regarding our olive trees. We couldn't decide if they were extending our grant for the trees or taking it away. I scrabbled for my Spanish-to-English dictionary, lurking somewhere deep in my huge handbag. Then we heard a male voice, with an Essex accent, behind us.

"Are you Pete and Diane from the *campo*?"

"Yes that's us," we said in unison, turning around.

The couple, sitting at another table, got up and introduced themselves.

"I'm Andy and this is Julie. We've heard that you've had a bit of trouble."

He pulled up a chair.

"Word gets out," Julie said, with a comforting smile, also pulling up a chair.

We told them how we had become reluctant trainee goat herders. Julie and I bonded over horses, Andy and Pete bonded over the madness of Spanish paperwork, then we all bonded over a bottle of wine.

They had bought their *finca* (rural property) just outside the town in 2002. Andy still had a job in England and they commuted between England and Spain. The next year, during the hottest month of summer, they took down the *finca's* roof.

Andy was offered early retirement and in 2004 they moved over permanently. Now they had time to renovate their house in earnest. They lived about seven kilometres upriver from us and understood that living close to a river was wonderful, but also very dangerous.

"So, let's sum this up," said Andy. "You're using a portaloo, a camp stove, and a shower bag for a scrub?"

"Yes," I said. "Money is a bit tight at the moment so we are making do."

"Right, I see. I'll be down at the weekend to cost a shower room, kharzi and a kitchen." Kharzi was his slang term for a loo.

Julie saw the panic in my eyes.

"It's okay Diane," she said. "We will cost the materials and then you know what you are looking at. But you have to have the basics."

She was right of course. Camping out in the summer months is easy and fun. But come winter, not so much.

Antonio had told us that we had to sow our big field, which is about two and a half acres, with mixed grasses for the goats to eat in the spring. We bought the seeds and ploughed the field with the tractor. These grasses would help the girls produce a good amount of milk and then, maybe, we could actually make some money.

Meanwhile we decided that the last of our savings should be used to build the basics. Andy and Julie were waiting for the call and started work.

Half an old building, opposite the main house, was converted into a shower and toilet. The other half was to be used as a bedroom. A kitchen was built in the main house and a septic tank put in place. To drag the farm into the modern world, all we needed now was a steel tower for the water tank.

By December, 2009, we were doing rain dances. We needed more rain. It was Antonio who'd thought that running around in a circle, doing a rain dance, would somehow help. It seemed to work because there was a steady fall a week before Christmas.

The river was swollen and we couldn't cross a bridge to graze our animals on the far hills. However, we could walk over Antonio's land which was closer to home. On Christmas Eve we ventured to a spot we had saved for the goats' Christmas Dinner. To get there, we needed to jump across a small gorge with brambles growing over it.

By 5 pm the rain began to get heavier so it was time to turn the goats and head for home. It was sticky going as the herd had turned the pathway into a muddy bog. Jumping over the gorge and ducking down under the brambles was tricky. Two inches of mud clung to my Wellington boots and my glasses were steamed up, making it a tad dangerous.

I did it with the help of a few swear words to give me a rocket boost and forgetting that Santa may have been listening. The goats ran the rest of the way back to their stables. By the time I arrived at Antonio's sheds, my girls had already disappeared down the track for home. We wished each other a happy Christmas and then it dawned on me that something was missing.

"Where's Carmen?"

"She is probably with the goats. It's Christmas and she wants her feed. Don't worry."

Antonio wrestled with his shed door, his whole herd pushing him, trying to get in out of the rain.

But I *was* worried. Carmen never left me. Carmen, that tiny white bundle, had grown into a beautiful sheep. Not just any old sheep, but the most intelligent sheep in the whole world. She would never leave me alone on a track in the pouring rain. She knew how accident-prone I was. Hoping Antonio was right, I ran back to the farm, only falling twice.

"Is Carmen here?" I panted, praying for the right answer.

"No, she's with you, isn't she?"

Wrong answer.

"Oh no, oh no! She's probably in the bloody gorge! She might not have made the jump. Get another torch. I'm going to find her. Lock the girls down and follow me up." I paused for breath then shouted over my shoulder, "Bring a rope!"

I banged on Antonio's stable door, the rain now hammering down.

"Carmen?"

"Yes, Carmen. She's in the gorge. MOVE IT!"

As I took off along the hill track the light was nearly gone. I jogged, winding up my rechargeable torch at the same time.

"CARMEN!" I screamed, before stopping to listen.

I heard nothing. In the darkness, the sound of rushing water beneath me was scary.

"CARMEN!"

"Baaaaaa!"

She *was* in the gorge. I gave the torch a last wind, and tried to visualise the jump across the gorge as it would be in the day light.

"Just bloody do it, Diane. Jump!" I told myself.

I leapt, landed and flashed my torch. There she was, flat on her back stuck on a pile of bramble cuttings that a farmer had chucked into the gully. I couldn't move her. Looking up the hill I saw Pete's torch. Antonio was already running down the hill.

He must have done a flying leap at the gorge as he landed quite close to us. He hauled Carmen up the steep bank and on to the gorge where Pete was waiting with some rope. Thankfully we didn't need it.

"Get me home!" she baaad.

It took us another twenty minutes to get back to Antonio's sheds. The rain was hammering down and we could barely see a foot in front of us. We said our goodbyes then stopped to listen to the sound of the river. It was roaring now and the sound was frightening.

As soon as we arrived back at the farm, Carmen dashed to her pen, and we dashed inside to stoke the fire. Dry clothes on, we decided to enjoy a Spanish Christmas dinner at 11 pm. I had cooked a large chicken earlier in the day and bought prawns and ice cream for treats over Christmas. Starters and desserts!

Opening the freezer door, to defrost some of the prawns, we discovered that the gas fridge had stopped working and everything had defrosted. Christmas dinner comprised a large bag of prawns, sweetcorn, and sloppy ice cream. The chicken would have to wait.

At midnight we ventured outside again. The river had burst its banks and was crashing through our fields. All we could do was to empty the buckets we'd placed upstairs, to catch the leaks in the roof, and pray.

At first light we ventured out. The rain was still heavy and the river was moving fast across our fields. It brought large eucalyptus trees with it and drowned our spring grazing. The water was creeping closer and closer to the goat paddocks and the house.

A huge wash brought the water through our front paddock and into our store room. Our minds were racing. We had half a dozen mums with babies. We could cut our back fence and take the main herd up to Antonio's. But what to do with the rest?

I filled sacks full of straw and dashed upstairs to cobble together temporary pens for the mums. As long as they could dodge the leaks in the roof, they would be safe. I had already locked the horses in a paddock behind the house so they were quite safe from the river. All the dogs were inside, huddled by the fire.

I watched Pete as he stood in the front paddock. He was checking the depth-pole he had placed earlier in the field to see how quickly the river was moving towards the paddocks and house. I grabbed the wire-cutters and waited for him to give the signal to get the goats out and up to Antonio's. I saw him reach for his phone.

Andy had called from his *finca* upriver to tell Pete that the river was slowing down. The pole Pete had placed in the ground the night before, which had disappeared this morning, could now be seen. I put the wire-cutters back on the table and opened a bottle of wine. I didn't care that it was only 8 am. We both needed something and brandy was not available.

We gave the goats hay and enjoyed the Christmas chicken, without starters and dessert. The rain eased, then returned with a vengeance, only to ease again later.

Pete decided to sleep on a sun lounger by the fire, so that he could check the river on the hour throughout the night. We put all our fuel into the generator and kept it running. I went to bed to get a few hours sleep only to be woken by Pete half an hour later.

"Get up Di, you have to watch this."

Of course he was right to wake me. The film that was being played at 3 am, on Boxing Day morning, was *A Wonderful Life*. We munched on chocolate and laughed, cried, then laughed again.

It continued to rain for three months. Not only did we lose all our grazing, river banks, fencing and sprinkler system, we also lost the motor which pumps the water to our house. It was buried in river mud.

For the next few months we spent our fast dwindling savings on pipes that ran from a high gorge near Antonio's sheds down to our house. This kept us in water throughout the spring. Thanks to our friends, who had organised '*Campo* Aid', enough money was raised to repair our motor and clean out our well.

That Christmas taught us many things. An important lesson was always to have a bottle of brandy in the house. The upside was that the river had kindly dumped lots of firewood close to the house, ready to be cut for the following winter.

A year later the river came through again, right in the middle of birthing time.

3

Wasps and Snakes

The calypso tune on my phone springs into life.

"Where are you?" shouts Antonio, over his tractor's noisy engine.

"The lost garden. Everyone's asleep."

"Stay put a bit longer. You'll want to get to the *horno* around 5 pm. It's a furnace on the tracks. Take it slow."

The *horno*, Spanish for oven, is aptly named. It's just an uphill concrete road that winds on and on and there is no shade. Only at the end can we drop down to the river, or dash into an old olive grove. I have no intention of climbing it before 5 pm.

I look at Chinni. She opens one eye and fixes me with a stare, then closes it again. A few goats get up to drink from the river before quickly returning to the shade of the trees for another snooze. That's the trick for surviving in this intense heat. Keep still and switch off.

I sit next to Chinni, my back pressing up against a tree. All my girls shuffle closer to me, chewing the cud, their heads resting on their siblings' backs, farting freely.

Our herd had grown steadily. Antonio had helped by swapping boys for girls and if any of his goats gave birth to three or four, he gave me one. It was less work for him and less strain on the mum. Hildy, Sandra, Louise, Janet, Gerona and finally, little Mariposa, joined the herd.

"This is a little one you need to take, Diane. I have named her Mariposa (Butterfly). She is small but healthy."

Antonio held up a tiny brown kid, perfect but miniature.

"She needs help to reach a teat and I have too many to cope with," he said, shoving Mariposa into my arms.

Lucy was the best choice for the little one to feed on. She was very calm and loved babies. Peter held Mariposa up to her teat and she drank a full side. Mariposa wouldn't accept a bottle so our nights were long. Poor Lucy had to get up at 2 am, still half asleep, and stand while I or Peter, also half asleep, held up the baby to feed. We kept her in a box next to our bed and after three weeks she was able to feed by herself. Thanks to Lucy she grew and thrived.

Lucy adopted orphaned, rejected or weak babies. She always aborted late in her pregnancies and this saddened us. Being unable to have her own kid, she loved every baby we presented for her to take care of.

"Lucy is a treasure to you, Diane," said Antonio. "Don't worry that she can't have babies. She will be worth her weight in gold."

And so she is.

The naming game became a competition with Antonio. I named one of my babies India, so he promptly named one of his Africa. Next came Canada, so he named one of his Americana. These babies, now fully grown, were all sleeping around me, quiet and content, apart from the odd fly or wasp.

If only I had listened to the old Spanish saying, I may have had a clue that the winter of 2009 was going to be a wet one. The saying goes, the year of the wasp is the year of mud. It works better in

Spanish but it means that if you have a lot of wasps in spring and summer, expect heavy rains in the winter.

Peter can cope with the various creepy-crawlies that we have living with us at the farm. Scorpions, snakes, rats and spiders are all a piece of cake. But wasps, no. I have seen him calmly send a scorpion that had climbed onto the kitchen work surface to its maker. Later, however, faced with a wasp, he flaps his arms, squeals, and runs around in circles, like a teenager that finds a row of spots on her face before a date.

To be fair, the wasps in Spain are vicious brutes. They build their nests in door frames, in holes in bricks, or beneath garden chairs. In fact they have a housing complex just about anywhere we happen to be on the farm, They stake their claim and attack anyone who passes by.

The summer before the floods the wasps were everywhere. We armed ourselves with cans of wasp spray. They would flash out of their nests and we had to be quick on the draw with our spray cans. Then we would go in for the kill, squirting the nest. Running inside, we applied the latest 'this will take the pain out of a wasp sting' cure onto burning parts of our bodies. Wine, vinegar, olive oil and assorted creams were purchased from the chemist. None worked.

I climbed out of bed very early, one particular Sunday morning, as there was lots to be done before the heat set in. I swung open the front door and was met by a solid wall of wasps hovering outside. I felt like I was in a Hitchcock film and quickly slammed the door closed.

"Bugger off!" I shouted.

With my early morning logic I thought that slamming the door and shouting might have scared them off. I gingerly opened the door again. Nope, they were still there and buzzing even more loudly.

"How do I tell Pete?" I asked the fridge, pressing my head against the door.

"What the hell is going on?" asked Pete, emerging from the bedroom and making his way to the front door to go out for a pee.

I leapt in front of the door and spread my arms wide.

"You can't go outside. Get dressed. You need long sleeves and boots."

"I need to bloody pee!" His eyes had started to bulge.

"Wasps, Peter, an army of bloody wasps are outside. Don't open the door. I repeat, do not open the door."

Pete opened the door.

Any thoughts of relieving himself vanished as he walked backwards into the room, eyes fixed and wide.

"Full body armour, Peter. We're under siege and I don't think a deal is on the table with this lot."

Minutes later we were dressed in our rain gear. Wellington boots, rubber gloves and sun glasses. With a can of wasp spray in each hand we had turned into Butch Cassidy and the Sundance Kid, but hopefully with a better ending. I muttered the line, "Next time I say let's go to Bolivia, let's go to Bolivia!" Then on the count of three, we opened up both doors and let rip.

"Watch out behind you, Pete."

"I've got him. Clear to the left."

"Above your head Pete, I'm nearly out of ammo."

We ducked, dived and twirled, spraying everything in sight. As the last of the spray spluttered dry, the last of the wasps hit the ground. We high-fived and crunched our way back inside the house to look for the dust-pan and brush.

A few days later, I was introduced to another sort of wasp.

Antonio and I had walked for three hours to a field where a certain herb and wild cabbage grew. I had an umbrella to shade me from the blistering heat.

"Watch out for the ground wasps," Antonio said as we entered the field.

What on earth was he talking about? Ground wasps?

A few moments later I had my first attack. The goats were greedily munching herbs when the wasps erupted like roman candles on Bonfire Night. Goats, dogs and herders ran to the side of the field and took shelter in the long grass. When we felt that the coast was clear we ventured out again.

Four minutes or so would pass and another attack would occur. I used my umbrella as a shield but it only protected me for about three seconds before I ran into the long grass again. The goats had fled the field, they'd had enough. It was on the sixth attack, as I ran blindly into the tall weeds, that I came face to face with a huge wasps' nest.

Yet again, life was turning into a film. It was like the scene from *Aliens* when Ripley discovers the mother alien. Beautifully constructed, dome-shaped and around a metre high, it must have been a deluxe block of flats. I slowly backed away. Not having Ripley's flame gun, I called for the next best thing.

"Antonio, bring the sling-shot."

We stood at what we thought was a safe distance. Antonio prepared the sling shot. I found two good sized stones and handed him the first one. Antonio does not speak English but he perfectly understood my quiet instruction.

"Nuke 'em!"

The first shot took out the helipad and penthouse suite. The second took out the third and second floors. The wasps fell out in a confused daze before recovering themselves. They stopped panicking and turned to face us.

"RUN!" I shouted. All I saw was the dust that Antonio had already left behind.

The bastard didn't even look back.

Apart from the scorpions, we try to live harmoniously with all the creatures in the house. Such is their arrogance that they choose to ignore the large sign I wrote saying, 'Scorpions keep out, all intruders will be executed'. Either that or, being Spanish, they don't understand English. Anyway, those that do enter, Peter dispatches very quickly.

Peter's son, Arthur, came to stay and walked around the house in his socks. I gently suggested that he always wear his trainers and to check the insides before slipping his feet into them.

"You never know when scorpions are around," I explained.

I didn't want to scare him and didn't want to nag. Being a teenager he paid little heed. He managed to survive the week without being stung, falling off a cliff or being scared witless by large snakes in the goat sheds.

When we got home, after taking him to the airport, we cleared away his makeshift bed only to find a scorpion lurking just where he kept his trainers.

Snakes are very shy. They are happy to potter about keeping the mice and rat population down without disturbing us. Occasionally we cross paths as they wriggle across the stable floor. We greet them politely and carry on with our day. Then Graham moved into House Two.

Until we win the lottery, we use House Two as a hay store/tool shed. It's very cool in the summer and the dogs and special-needs goats like to sleep in there. At night we have to slalom around their slumbering forms to turn off the generator which is on the upper floor.

We spotted a snake gliding in and out of the hay bales and rejoiced that we now had a mouse catcher in House Two. We named him Graham. He seemed to be non-aggressive and allowed us to address him as a house guest.

Then one hot summer evening, when Pete climbed the stairs to turn off the generator, we discovered Graham had a sense of humour and evidently enjoyed *Pink Panther* movies. Graham turned into Cato.

As Pete opened the door at the bottom of the stairs Graham fell onto his neck. He then slid down Pete's body, naked except for boxer shorts, and slowly wriggled over Pete's curling toes before disappearing into the hay bales.

We decided, after Peter had murdered a triple brandy, that it was a one-off. He must have been resting on top of the door frame. How wrong we were.

A few days later I walked into House Two to fetch a broom.

Graham, never one to let the opportunity of a good practical joke pass him by, fell off the hay stack onto my shoulder, before gleefully gliding down to plop onto my flip flops.

No matter how careful we were, he managed to out-smart us. Once he disguised himself as a garden hose, only to come alive as we passed by.

"Eeeeeyaaaa!" he cried, heading for a hole in the hay stack.

"Ooooeeeeyaaaaaa!" he screamed, as he fell off the outside of the door frame and onto my arm.

As winter drew near, Graham disappeared. The hay was getting low and mice pickings were getting scarce. The following summer Pete had popped into House Two to make up the goat feed while I made early morning tea. He walked into the kitchen visibly shaken.

"Whatever is the matter?" I asked, shoving a mug of over-brewed tea into his hand.

"He's back."

"Who's back?"

"Graham… and he's grown."

4

Rumble in the Jungle

Chinni starts to stir so it's time to move on. The heat is relentless. Not a whisper of a breeze in the air. The only creatures oblivious to the heat, apart from the pesky flies, are the bee-eaters. In a flash of harlequin colour they dart in and out of their nest holes in the river bank, seemingly unaware of the outside furnace.

Chinni moves higher to a small cliff crossing where the track doubles back down to the river bed. She scans the herd to make sure everyone is up and ready. I gather my leftover lunch into my rucksack and do battle with Alice. She insists there is an orange somewhere at the bottom of the bag.

Climbing up to Chinni I wonder if I should start calling the goats that are still grazing in the river bed. I think better of it as she is now in control. My voice might cause another stampede. She knows what she is doing, she is the herd leader.

Chinni had always lived in the shadow of Alice and Pepita. Alice, a Payoya breed, brown with a speckle of white, tough, horned, bloody-minded, is a bully. Pepita, a different breed, is half Granadina with a touch of Payoya. Unlike Alice, Pepita had no horns. She is tall, black and peace-loving. They are the best of friends.

Alice bullied everyone. To get at the best feeding spot at the troughs she smashed goats aside. She horned sleeping goats out of the good spots for shade. Everyone hated her except me and, of course, Pepita. There were those who could take Alice on but, knowing she had a secret weapon, they left her well alone.

The secret weapon was Pepita. Despite her gentle non-aggresive nature, Pepita turned into a prize-fighter if anyone upset Alice. Her size and weight gave her an advantage but it was her skill and focus that made her a formidable opponent in a fight.

"Trouble brewing," said Antonio as we walked along a narrow path on a hillside.

"What's happening?" I asked, keeping my eyes fixed on the path and trying not to fall down to a rocky olive grove below.

"Alice is shoving my goats off the path."

I scuttled forward and peered over Antonio's shoulder. Yep, there she was, pushing and tipping any goat walking in front of her.

"My lot will ambush her in the olive grove," he said, stopping to roll a cigarette. "She won't get away with this. You wait and see."

He was right. As Alice climbed down the path to munch on some old olive branches, three of Antonio's big-horned girls surrounded her.

"Where's Pepita?" I frantically searched the hillside.

"Right behind you."

Pepita was munching bracken and watching. The three goats pushed and shoved Alice, horns trying to lock onto her legs.

"Do something Antonio," I pleaded. "They'll murder her."

"About time too," he said, as he lit his roll-up and leaned back against a bank to watch the fight.

Pepita calmly carried on eating with one eye on her friend.

"Need a hand there, Alice?" she called out.

Pepita had turned into her alter ego, The Sundance Kid.

"Now would be a good idea, Peps," her friend, Butch Cassidy, replied, dodging another horn attack below the knee.

Pepita walked calmly off the track and down into the olive grove. Without pausing, her head went down to deliver a blow into the side of goat number one, sending it rolling down the bank. Goat number two took too long to get into position. She half reared up to meet the big black she-devil charging towards her. With a shoulder charge worthy of Vinnie Jones, Pepita sent her sprawling down the bank with her tail between her legs. Goat number three backed away.

"Ain't got no quarrel with you, Pepita," the goat muttered. "No quarrel with you at all."

Alice walked to Pepita's side.

"If she comes back, Peps, put her over the cliff," whispered Alice.

"Love to," said Pepita, reaching to grab a mouthful of olive.

"Alice is lucky to have Pepita," Antonio said, a little disappointed.

Pepita loved youngsters and never minded if they jumped on and off her back while she sunned herself. However, she disliked one of Antonio's water dogs, named Pirri, as he had zero patience with young goats in the *campo*.

If a young kid ventured into an olive grove, the other dogs would gently nuzzle the babies off the trees. But Pirri nipped them. He was feared by all the goats. Not one goat challenged him and only the big Spanish Mastiff dogs could keep him in order.

One hot evening we were walking the goats down a long dusty track. Antonio was in the lead, guarding olive trees, and I was working my way slowly back to the middle of the grazing herd, checking the trees to my right. Suddenly I heard the scream of a baby. I started to run. It had to be one of mine. My girls stood stock still.

"He's bitten Milly's kid!" the goats shouted to each other.

As I paused for breath, hands resting on my knees, Pepita galloped passed me. It was as if she had turned into a raging black bull with her head down and nostrils flaring. Pirri, who had now sat down under an olive tree, didn't see her coming.

Having caught my breath, I continued to jog down the track and then watched in wonder as Pepita sent him into orbit. He tried to get to his feet but she was just too quick for him. She kept charging until she had sent him on his way. By the time I got to there, Pirri was running for the safety of Antonio's herd. The goats cheered my big, beautiful girl.

Pepita died a year later. It was sudden and Pete cradled her head as her heart stopped beating. To this day I don't know why. What did I miss? What did I miss? It broke our hearts but it was Alice we felt for. She had lost her best friend and protector.

Alice continued to bully the rest of the herd, but kept close to me for protection. Chinni meanwhile was growing in strength. She had shaken off her many illnesses and was ready to take on Alice and become the herd leader. It had always been her ambition. Antonio watched her try to force her way to the front of the herd but she could never get past his big girls. Just when we thought she might succeed, she got sick again.

One hot sticky afternoon I was walking my girls downriver. I had the valley to myself. With the help of Peter and others, Antonio had moved to the mill. The girls were happily munching in the river bed and I had found a shady spot to read my book. Alice sat close.

We shared my lunch and she was happily eating the last of my oranges when Chinni came and sat on the other side of me. Alice lifted her head, got up and moved nearer. Chinni also got up and moved closer to me. I could see Alice trying to work out what to do next. Placing my book gently back into my rucksack, I sat still and waited to see how this would play out.

Alice stood up, twisting and stretching her neck. The goats stopped eating by the river and jostled for a ringside seat. Chinni slowly got up and faced Alice. Who would make the first move? I dragged my rucksack into the cane reeds that line the river bank, keeping well out of the way of this battle. The fight was on.

Alice reared up and came down on Chinni's horns. On and on she hit her with all her might. Rearing, head butting, pushing and slamming into Chinni, who kept moving fast, ducking and weaving. Alice was short, stocky and mean. Chinni was tall, graceful and calculating. This was the 'Rumble in the Jungle'.

I sat very still and prayed that no one would break a leg. On and on they fought as dust swirled up and momentarily hid the boxers. When it cleared, Alice was still slamming into her. Chinni shook her head. Maybe she had sand in her eyes or maybe she was just teasing. Then they locked horns. Alice pushed with all her strength but Chinni held her. In that moment Chinni became Muhammad Ali and Alice was George Foreman.

And then it dawned on me. Chinni was letting Alice punch herself out. She was using the rope-a-dope.

With the perfect timing that only a true champion can possess, Chinni leaned in close.

"Is that all you've got, Alice?" she whispered.

It was. Alice had tired herself out and had nothing left. They unlocked horns and Chinni waited. It was all over, Alice had quit on her stool at the end of the eighth round. She turned to sit by me and Chinni turned and walked to the river.

She had not humiliated Alice by chasing her away from me or the herd, which is normal when a battle takes place. This was not personal. It was a calculated take over.

She was now the Queen and all the goats breathed a sigh of relief. For the following year Chinni was the most amazing leader, not only taking care of the herd, but me and Pete too. Then illness struck again.

5

Antonio Makes a Mistake

Antonio is on his noisy tractor when he phones me.

"Are you close to Diego's cliff?" he shouts into his mobile, above the roar of the engine.

"Yes, just moving towards it now."

"Remember to watch the kids. Don't let them go up the cliff. Oh, and the new orange trees planted across the river. Guard them with your life."

"Right, so you want me to be in two places at the same time?"

"*Claro*. Of course!"

I really can't think of any response to this so I just hold the phone to my ear and wait. He is obviously doing the same thing. He folds first.

"Are the *machos* behaving themselves?"

"All quiet so far," I reply. "Bruce Lee and Julio are just starting to sniff at the teenagers."

"That's okay. They won't cause any trouble until dusk."

With that the line goes dead.

A *macho* is the name given to a male goat. At that time he had five. With the exception of Julio, all were named after boxers or martial arts experts. Bruce Lee, Rocky, Jackie Chan, Cassius Clay.

Antonio loves martial arts. While the goats munch on the hillside, during our walks, he practices his Kung Fu on old olive tree branches.

He will seek out a worthy opponent. Facing the olive tree he places his hands together and bows low. The olive tree rattles its leaves and assumes a 'crouching tiger' position. Antonio favours the 'cobra' stance. He hitches up his trousers, twists his neck, then disarms (or rather dismembers) the tree with either a karate chop or a high kick. Dead branches are then collected and placed under a bush for future camp fires.

"Next time it rains, Pedro, you can drive us to Campillos to pick up a couple of babies. It's time for some new blood in the herd."

Antonio has a way of telling us what to do with our time. It's pointless arguing with him. As yet we have not mastered the art of tutting and sucking our teeth, as the Spanish do, to say, 'I think not'. Once his mind is made up he assumes we will go along with his plan which, of course, we do.

Two days later we found ourselves on the road to Campillos, a town half an hour's drive from Olvera. The rain was bucketing down. Back home, the goats would be lucky to get an hour's feed time.

I had imagined, on a wet day like this, that I would light an early fire and prepare the dinner. The generator purring away and washed clothes drying on the airer above the wood-burner would be my idea of heaven.

Instead, we were trying to find a farm track in a sheet of rain that the windshield wipers can barely cope with. Antonio, having no sense of direction outside of Olvera, kept waving his hand to the right.

"It's somewhere over there, Pedro."

Thankfully Pete has a brilliant sense of direction and he slowly trundled the car up a muddy track to a huge farm. It had an intensive goat unit, something I had never seen before. A swarthy-looking chap met us at the doorway and bundled us into the first barn.

"Follow me," he said, and took off at a brisk pace.

We trotted behind him, glancing at the few hundred goats lying to the left of the walkway. They were in brilliant condition, snuggled down in deep, clean straw with gentle lighting overhead. They all looked content and were chewing the cud. I wondered if the older ones handed down stories to their kids, of how they used to walk the hills and valleys and felt the sun on their backs.

We finally came to the baby unit. There were countless kids under heat lamps, others in big crèches. These were pure Malaguenian goats. Antonio scuttled from pen to pen, searching for the best two to buy. He finally picked out the two boys he wanted and (with a nod and a wink) money quickly changed hands.

The babies were put into a big cardboard box and we were ushered out to our car. There was no time to take a peek at the kids until we got back to the farm. However, the rain had eased so we made good time getting back to our track.

We transferred the box to Antonio's Land Rover and we got the boys out to take a good look at them. Antonio was like a child on Christmas morning, opening his first gift.

"Look! Look at the blonde one! He has a Chinese mark on the side of his cheek. I will name him Bruce Lee. Welcome to Las Vicarias."

The next boy was a bright chestnut colour.

"Feel, feel. He is going to have horns! I name him Julio."

"Julio? Why Julio?"

"Name of the best dog in the world." he said, his eyes misting over. "It was before your time here."

And so Bruce Lee and Julio were taken to their new home. It was that night, for the first time that I had known and worked with him, that Antonio made a huge mistake. Rule number one: never introduce a new animal into the herd without first isolating it for a few weeks. He/she might have an illness that could infect the other goats.

The next morning Pete and I popped up to Antonio's sheds, after we had finished milking our girls, to see how the boys were settling in. Entering a shed we saw Bruce Lee and Julio jumping on and off Antonio's back while he milked a goat.

"Why are the boys out of their pen?" I yelled at him. "Are you crazy?"

He shuffled over to us, bent double. Julio was balancing on his shoulders.

"It was so cold last night I brought them down from the top stable and made a fire for them to keep warm." He pointed at a smouldering pile of olive wood.

"Well, if all the goats get sick then it will be your fault!"

I stomped out of the shed and walked back home, leaving Peter to coo over the boys, making up for his wife's outburst of temper.

Within a week all his goats got an eye infection which, of course, spread to my herd. When the milk cheque arrived, half of it was spent on medication. Hours were lost putting drops into eyes. As we finished our lot we would dash up to help Antonio medicate his two hundred.

It was pointless crying over spilled milk. The damage was done and we had to get on with it. Some goats responded quickly to the drops, others took longer. We separated the unaffected goats as best we could but it was pointless. They would all be together when we walked them in the afternoon.

One cold, wet, windy day, Antonio and I took the goats high on the hills where there were some fresh herbs. We were slowly making our way back down again when the rain got heavier. The goats began to trot and it was a race to get to the bottom before they did. We didn't want them crossing a small bridge without supervision. Antonio was ahead of me and looked up.

"Diane!" he shouted above the howling wind, "get to Chinni. She has gone blind!"

I scanned the herd and there she was, stumbling and falling down the hill above me. I ran up as fast as I could.

"It's okay, Chinni! I'm coming!"

She stood still, moving her head from side to side, listening for my voice. I searched inside my rucksack for the collar and lead that I always carried for such emergencies. Reaching her, I gently slipped on the collar.

"Just trust me, Chin," I said, placing my hand on her neck and her face touched my leg. "Let's go home. Nice and slowly."

Goats were dashing past us wanting to get to the warm sheds. Antonio hurried to the bridge to get them across safely. I phoned Pete, sheltering the phone under my coat. I gave him garbled instructions to go to Antonio's sheds and collect our herd.

By the time Chinni and I had reached the makeshift bridge, all the goats had crossed and were running up the steep track for home. All except Carmen the sheep. She had made sure all our girls had crossed safely and then waited for me. She didn't trust the bridge or my ability to cross it with a sick goat.

"It's okay, Carmen!" I shouted. "Go with the girls!"

With Chinni out of action, she now had to make sure that all of our girls would separate from Antonio's herd. I watched her big white rump disappearing up the track before turning my attention to the problem at hand.

The bridge is made from three eucalyptus branches tied together. Old grain sacks, filled with sand, are placed on top for the goats to walk on. The river was rising quite quickly and in twenty minutes it would be over the bridge. I decided the best way to cross was for me to walk backwards with Chinni's head leaning into my legs and my hands on either side of her face.

The river was making a heck of a din and Chinni snorted. I slowly moved one leg backwards. No words were needed. She had worked it out. As my leg moved, so did hers. We carefully crossed the bridge with tiny steps. Mirroring my every move, we became Fred Astaire and Ginger Rogers.

Safely on the other side, we now had to climb the steep and muddy track up to Antonio's sheds. It took an hour to finally get home. We were both cold and wet and very anxious. Pete had already prepared a pen for her and stayed with her, holding her food as she ate.

I thought it best to leave her. Messing about in the dark stable would only distress her. This was not the time to begin sorting out a blind goat. We were all exhausted and tomorrow would come soon enough.

The following morning the sun had come out. After milking we moved Chinni to a small, safe paddock with a cool stable attached. It butted onto the main paddock so she was still close to the herd. I walked her round and round the corral, familiarising her with the fencing and the water bucket. After half an hour she could manage on her own.

She always stood like a rock when I put in two lots of eye drops. She had to have them three times a day. All I had to say was, "medicine time," and she stood still, lifting her head up for me.

Was this because she was the most perfect patient? No. She was a survivor, plain and simple. She didn't want to lose her crown because she was blind and she knew I was sorting out the problem. Patience and determination are the things that have kept her going throughout her life.

It took nearly a month to fully restore her sight. During that time I let the girls enter the adjoining paddock to see her. They needed to know that Chinni was still in charge.

Trouble, however, was brewing within the herd. Big Suzanna was taking full advantage of Chinni's absence. She began by taking over the best sleeping pallet that Alice and her family always used. Then she bullied Hildy, biting her ear at every opportunity.

The other goats were nervous. Taking on Alice and Hildy was showing the rest of the girls that she wasn't afraid of the big guns. Things came to a head when she hooked Willow's front leg and broke it. It was the first time I'd had to splint a broken leg, without Antonio giving instructions, double-checking I had done it correctly.

Chinni understood what was happening within the herd though. She got all the information she needed from Willow who was recuperating in the next stable.

"It was that bloody Suzanna who did this to me. She needs sorting out!"

Willow was never the most refined of goats. Had she been a human teenager she would definitely have been a punk rocker.

The next morning I let the girls into the paddock next to Chinni. Peter and I watched as Suzanna walked with a confident swagger up to the dividing fence. Chinni waited until Suzanna started to head butt the fence.

Then in a flash Chinni stuck her nose through the wire and grabbed Suzanna's ear. She pulled back with all her might, teeth firmly clamped. Suzanna's scream echoed throughout the valley. It was time for Chinni to return to the herd. She was ready.

Bruce Lee and Julio became spoilt brats, demanding to sit on our laps and share our packed lunches. Antonio continued to indulge their every whim. By the time they were eight months old their characters had formed.

Bruce Lee was gentle and respectful. He understood his place within the *macho* world of *machos*. Julio, on the other hand, grew a magnificent pair of horns and wanted to try them out by pushing for fights with the older chaps. He lost every bout. He needed a trainer and she lived at Las Vicarias.

A year after Rafael had dumped Carmen outside our front door, he left another surprise.

"A gift of a lamb for you English," he called through our window.

I dashed outside, saw the bundle and made a feeble attempt to shout to the little Spaniard who was racing back to his car.

"I don't need another bloody sheep!"

Pete cuddled the lamb and named her Loretta. She was a different breed to Carmen and spoke to us in a slow West-country accent. Carmen had developed a low, rich operatic voice. They couldn't have been more different. Carmen was highly intelligent, Loretta was very slow on the uptake.

In the art of fighting, however, she was a walking tank. There is not an animal on the farm that can take on Loretta in a fight. Goats twirl, rear and dance, Loretta runs and rams.

Julio moved into Las Vicarias and used her like a punch bag, pounding and pushing her. Loretta loved it and he grew in strength and stamina.

I needed to scrub the house as my daughter, Felicity, was arriving in a few days and the place was covered in dust. Antonio agreed to collect my girls and walk them with his lot. I waved them goodbye and set to work.

Living in an old ruin with no glass in the windows has been a challenge for me. In England I was a dust fanatic and I would drive my daughters mad. They might be engrossed in the latest episode of *Buffy the Vampire Slayer* and I would spot a shadow over the television screen. I would granny-dance, bent double, shuffling to see the offending layer of dust, and rub frantically with my sleeve to clean it. Skirting-boards would get the daily finger test and walking upstairs I had to carry a cloth to wipe as I stepped. Complete madness.

Living here, it really is a matter of holding one's nerve. Mopping the floor is a weekly chore as water is always a concern, especially in the summer. Recycling all waste water is routine. Showers become a luxury. A large bowl is placed in the shower tray and enough water is dribbled in to soap up. Then a smidgeon of water is used to soap down. The bowl is then emptied into the mop bucket or used to flush the loo.

Occasionally, without warning, we get a visit from a friend who kindly brings food or discarded clothing for us. A honk on their car horn outside our gates is enough to send us into a panic. I wave at the gate then dash into the loo and flush. Then I rush back to the kitchen for a cloth, still waving at our friends. They are watching the weird spectacle of me rushing to and from the house, with a fixed grin and flapping my arms about.

Pete clears the dining table of bailing twine, goat books and dust. I clean the bathroom sink then look for a bra. Our friends now don't quite know what to do. To amuse them, I pass by again doing a funny dance and quickly check to see if the underwear drying on the backs of the chairs has been scooped up by Peter.

Only then can we let them in. I offer no explanation for the antics and delay and they do not ask. Peter mused that perhaps they thought they had caught us in a romantic clinch and they were a tad embarrassed. Personally, I think they've become accustomed to our eccentric behaviour. Either that or they think we're completely bonkers.

At 6 pm I tootled up the track to pick up the girls. They had separated from Antonio's herd without a hitch and Julio was proudly stepping out alongside them.

"You are not to handle Julio any more, Diane," Antonio said, fishing in his pockets for his tobacco.

"And why is that?"

"The bastard nearly stabbed me in the side today with his horns."

He lifted up his torn shirt to show me scrape marks on his waist.

"Julio attacked you?" I was astonished.

"Yes, first time ever a *macho* has turned on me. He wouldn't let me walk in front of him, he turned and charged."

Antonio was very upset that one of his boys could actually attack him.

"I'll come down for him tomorrow. He's far too dangerous for you to handle."

He spat out his roll-up and walked over to Bruce Lee and patted him on the head.

I decided not to tell Pete about Julio's antics. I imagined hearing his lecture: "If Antonio says he is dangerous then he is bloody dangerous. Let him deal with the little shit." No, it was best to keep quiet and sort the brat out in the morning.

Antonio rarely, if ever, disciplines any animals. He believes in praising good behaviour and ignoring bad behaviour. Quite right but he takes it a bit too far because he reasons with them. If a dog chases one of his precious chickens his response is: "Now that's naughty. What did little Reme do to upset you? Why can't you be friends?"

Antonio is also a master at blaming everyone else for his animal's shortcomings. I knew he would already be having the following conversation with Bruce Lee: "You are a good boy because you live with me. Julio is a bad boy because he lives with Diane and she and that fat sheep have ruined him!"

The following day I set off up the track with the herd, half an hour before Antonio was due to come down to fetch Julio. Just as I reached the place where Julio had attacked him, the wretch barged past me, before turning and starting to swing his horns. To be clear on what happened next, bucks in rut do not feel pain.

I quickened my pace and just as he lowered his horns to charge at me I ran up the side of the hill before turning on him, swinging my walking stick. Julio formulated the words *what the f—?* and before he reached the f-word, I hit him on the tip of his horns and ran further up the hill.

At this point my girls thought it best to stay put and munch the herbs on the side of the track. Mother had gone mad, yet again. Julio spotted fat Pat in front of the herd and made a dash to claim her.

"Really, Julio? I mean, really?"

I ran at him swinging my stick as if it were a baseball bat.

Meanwhile, Antonio had arrived at his sheds and was leaning against his Land Rover, watching the mad woman fighting with the young *macho*. Julio blinked, turned and quietly walked up to the sheds.

I thought it best to finish the whole thing off by chasing him up the hill with the sound of some choice, but particularly colourful, Anglo-Saxon ringing in his ears. Both of us arrived out of breath, Julio embarrassed and I victorious.

"Well now, that was interesting," Antonio said, throwing me an orange. "Discipline, the English way."

I noted he had a big smile on his face as he walked away.

6

Cliffs

Chinni and I stand side by side, weighing up the next leg of our journey. Ahead of us is the narrow path leading back down to the river. Above is a cliff and this is the place that Antonio is worried about.

Babies, being babies, love playing high on the rocks and cliffs. The older ladies are not interested. Why expend energy bouncing from one boulder to the next when there is a perfectly good path.

Many times Antonio has had to climb up a cliff and guide young goats and babies down while I hold the herd in the river bed below.

What to do?

Chinni has already made the decision and places herself at the foot of the cliff.

“Good plan, Chin. I’ll get going before this lot knock me off the path.”

I trot as fast as I can. I mustn’t let two hundred-odd impatient goats push past or send me crashing onto the rocks and brambles below. Just as my feet touch the lush river-bed grass, Tulipan, Antonio’s big *macho*, knocks me off my feet. I sprawl, then quickly curl up like a jockey thrown from his horse. The goats jump over me to get at the rich pickings of grass and oranges. I quickly stand.

"Don't you bloody dare cross that river!" I shout, spitting out sand.

A miracle happens. They all stop dead.

I turn to see if any babies have ducked past Chinni to get to the cliff-face 'playground'. There she stands, shaking her horns with a clear message for them to move on down the path. Not one passes her. I don't have to climb.

I have always been scared of heights. Then there is that strange feeling of being drawn to the edge of a steep drop even though every cell in your body is screaming, *are you completely bonkers?*

Pete has the same problem. In England, his job as a theatre technician required him to climb tall ladders to adjust lights for the stage. He would come home feeling a bit queasy. He couldn't work out if it was the lighting bar or his ladder that was moving.

He now suffers from vertigo, which can be a tad tricky, especially when Antonio phones for help.

"Good morning. I've got a goat stuck on the cliff by the sheds and I need a hand and some muscle. Thank you."

The phone goes dead and I have to pass this message onto Pete. I thought it best not to give him the full details.

"Antonio needs some muscle. Can you pop up?"

Feeling guilty, I accompany him.

"He said something about a goat and a cliff but I couldn't clearly understand. You know how he is."

Pete wasn't fooled for a moment. He knew that Antonio would only call if it was a very difficult situation. When we arrived at the sheds we saw Antonio in the distance standing on the edge of a cliff. It was a sheer drop. There would be no coming back if anybody fell down that. Pete blanched.

"Oh, holy shit," he said, looking at the path and then down at his boots.

Our financial situation meant that our boots were very well worn. Pete's boots had no tread left and he was unable to replace them for at least another month. We arrived at the cliff edge and his feet were already sliding beneath him.

"This is not going to be easy," said Antonio, when Pete finally skated up to him. "She is under the overhang, one false move and she will get spooked and fall."

Peter crouched down, not trusting his vertigo or his boots to hold him upright. This was going to be very tricky indeed. Antonio spat out his roll-up. He pulled out his sling-shot which was always hooked through his belt.

"I'll make a loop and lasso her. You hold me and we can pull her up and over the edge of the cliff. We've got one shot at this, Pedro."

Pete searched for something to tie around Antonio's waist.

"Just hold onto my belt while I lean over," Antonio said, full of confidence in Pete's strength.

"I'll pop back and get a rope from the shed," Pete suggested. "It'll be safer for you."

"No time. She will panic soon. Just hold onto me."

He edged towards the overhang and Pete grabbed his belt.

"Ready? I'm going for it now."

He dropped the lasso and deftly hooked the noose over the goat's horns. He pulled the loop tight and lifted her onto her back legs.

"Okay, pull," he said, with no trace of anxiety in his voice.

Peter pulled on Antonio's belt, praying it would hold. Antonio shuffled backwards and hauled the goat's shoulder over the cliff edge then stood up. Pete tried to stand without slipping.

"Grab her horns, Pedro!"

Pete knew if he slipped, all three would meet their maker. He let go of Antonio's belt and with a speed he later admitted he didn't know he had, grabbed the goat's horns and pulled. Antonio dug his boots firmly into the ground and grabbed her rump. Seconds later all four hooves were on the path.

He calmly removed the lasso from her horns and shooed her back to the sheds. Peter dropped to the ground. His boots were now taking on a life of their own and he didn't trust them not to dance off the cliff. Antonio sat next to him and rolled a cigarette.

"That could have been worse," he said, with his usual optimism.

"Yes," said Pete, snatching the roll-up and lighting it, "We could have died!"

"Ah, but we didn't."

"No, we didn't," said Pete, realising that although he had given up smoking, a near-death experience couldn't be counted as a relapse.

They both sat puffing away in silence for a few minutes.

"So, what's that bloody goat's name?" Peter asked.

"Lucky."

Boots then became a priority on our ever-growing list of priorities. My boots had worn a hole in the sole, but I was in luck. Antonio had bought a brand new pair and gave me his old ones. We have the same shoe size and his worn-out boots still had a month's tread in them.

This trade came with a price. I had to wear in his new left boot for a week. His foot was a tad wider than mine and needed my foot to make it supple. On this fine, warm day I skated and strode with him the long route to the *molino.*

It was the end of March, and hopefully we had seen the last of the storms. The river was still full and running fast. To enable the goats to cross the river and graze on fresh grass, Peter and Antonio had spent a few hours each day building new bridges. They used the trees that had fallen in the winter storms.

Without the use of a tractor or a four-wheel drive, they had to haul the logs using plain brute force. Between them they shuffled the log across the river, Antonio walking beside it with a rope. Once secured, the whole operation was repeated again. Then sacks were filled with sand and placed over the logs, providing a surface for the goats to cross. By the end of the week, three bridges had been built.

"Why are we going all the way to the *molino* today when there is plenty of food here?" I asked, having crossed the first bridge.

"I need to check the damage to the summer sheds. And anyway, the goats need some exercise."

We arrived at the last river crossing close to the old mill.

"We can't cross, Antonio. The big stones are gone and it's too wide to make a bridge."

"It's okay. We'll go via the cliff face."

"What! I think not, hombre!" I said, using my much-practiced Clint Eastwood stare.

A huge smile met my Clint stare.

"It will be fine, and at least you have one good boot to help you."

The cliff face is practically sheer. Normally, when we walked on this side of the river, we ambled along a low, cane-covered path. But that had been washed away and the parts remaining were thick mud. He ushered the goats up onto the higher ledge and he beckoned me to follow him onto a slightly lower one.

"Watch out for the stones that the goats will dislodge above us. The big ones could knock you off the path," he said, munching an orange.

I stared at the so-called pathway. It was barely the width of my foot. I told myself that it must get wider or else he wouldn't have risked taking me this way. It didn't and my stomach was in knots.

"Don't look down," he said. "Just follow me."

He stopped to avoid a shower of rocks falling from above. Of course I looked down.

"Antonio, STOP! It's Carmen. She's being dragged into the river. You have to help her!"

Carmen, my darling sheep, had continued along our normal path below, not realising that it had been washed away. She tried to turn back but the mud and the river currents were sucking her down and pulling her deeper into the water.

"Shit," muttered Antonio. "Stay put, I'll go and get her."

I wasn't planning on moving. My legs had turned to jelly. My heart rate had tripled with worry for Carmen and being alone on this sodding ledge. Antonio pulled her out of the mud and 'shooed' her up to the high ledge above me.

"She'll fall!" I shouted, almost in tears.

"No, she won't. Have faith."

He was right. She saw the goats in the distance and made a mad dash across the cliff face. I squinted above to see a white blob running as fast as her four legs could carry her.

To rescue Carmen, Antonio had to descend to the river then climb back up to be in front of me. It took quite a while for him to free-climb the rock face. I was rigid with fear. We continued to edge along when Antonio abruptly stopped.

"The next part is a bit tricky so go flat against the rock face."

Flat against the rock face meant that my heels were just over the edge of the ledge. Antonio shuffled his way back to me.

"Give me your arm."

I flung my right arm sideways, pressing my face into the cliff. He grasped my forearm and I clamped my hand around his. At that moment a film flashed through my mind.

"Antonio, do you remember that film called *Cliffhanger* with Sylvester Stallone?" I whispered.

"Oh yes, the one where he held that lady and…" His voice trailed off. "Look it's fine. You have one good boot and I have hold of you. Now, when I tell you to, stretch over, just feel your way across because part of the ledge has dropped off."

I closed my eyes.

"Dropped off?"

Dear heaven. It was then that Antonio's words finally struck me.

"Antonio, you have hold of me. Who has hold of you?"

"Move, Diane. We have to find the goats."

He tugged at my arm and I shuffled sideways, the cliff scratching my face.

"Okay, lift your right leg and shuffle sideways. One big stretch and there you go."

I lifted, shuffled and stretched.

"Now, put your left foot next to your right foot. Ready, now stretch."

I did as instructed, eyes closed and with very shallow breathing.

"You're fine now. Turn sideways and look for the goats."

Four more paces and the ridge widened into a path. The goats were grazing a little way down the hill but Carmen had waited for me under an olive tree. I looked back at the cliff then grabbed my water bottle from my rucksack. My tongue was stuck to the roof of my dry mouth. A few glugs later and I could speak.

"I can't do that again. I'd rather swim across the bloody river."

"You don't have to," he said. "We can climb up the other hill and get past the river that way. It will put fifty minutes on our journey but the grazing is good."

"Wait, wait! You mean we could have gone a different route?" I spluttered.

"Look, only two people that I know of have climbed that ridge. Me and now you. An experience Lady Dee. You did it."

He smiled, waiting for me to smile back.

"You bastard! You bloody Spanish bastard! I could have died!"

I actually stamped my foot while shouting this.

"Well, you didn't die and you are probably cured of your fear of heights."

He was right. I didn't die and I had crossed a ledge where only idiots and goats would venture. I could never be that scared again.

Could I?

7

Wells

The valley wakes up after siesta time. Birds stretch their wings and get ready to catch their afternoon food. Insects hover around the goats. Chinni and I move the girls across the river and into the cover of the thick, lush cane-grass. This will be their last rest before the dreaded 'oven' walk.

Chinni holds the goats in the cane while I run back to assist Sniffy and the Abuela across the makeshift bridge. The Abuela crosses first and waits for her friend.

Sniffy begins to push her invisible Zimmer frame onto the sacks of sand. Carefully she places her three good legs on the bridge and then swings her dodgy left hind one up to join them. It is painfully slow. One, two, three, swing and rest. One, two, three, swing and rest. She finally disembarks and bobs her way to the shade.

The Abuela stands still, watching her old friend. Or is she trying to remember who this goat is?

"Hello, who are you? Where am I?"

Bless her old bones. The Abuela has dementia.

Late one evening, the Abuela got mixed up with my goats when the herds separated after a long day's walk. We were feeding our girls their evening meals in two sittings. By the time Carmen and I had reached the corral, Pete had let the first bunch in and those in the second batch were impatiently waiting for their supper. I spotted the Abuela amongst them.

"What are you doing down here?" I asked her. "Antonio and your daughter will be worried."

Her eyes met mine.

"Is this the queue for dinner?"

"No dear, your dinner is up there."

I pointed in the general direction of Antonio's sheds.

"Is this the queue for dinner?" she asked again.

I phoned Antonio.

"I've got the Abuela and she really has lost the plot. I'm bringing her up now."

"Oh, I wondered why her daughter is standing by the *arroyo* (stream) looking your way." He paused then added, "Dementia may get us all in the end."

I gently put a collar around the Abuela's neck.

"Pete," I called, "I'm taking the old girl back to Antonio. She's come down here by mistake."

"Is this the queue for dinner?"

I slowly turned her towards the track.

"Come on sweetie, let's get you home."

She walks quietly behind me so there is no need to clip her on the lead. Her daughter has spotted her and comes trotting down to meet her with Antonio following.

"Is this the queue for dinner?" she asked Antonio, as he slowly walks towards her with a smile.

He bends down, undoes her collar and hands it to me. He places his hand on the old girl's neck.

"Madam, dinner awaits you. Come along."

The Abuela catches up with her friend, Sniffy, and both settle down in the shade, heads on each other's rumps. Chinni enjoys the oranges that I have liberated from old Diego's garden by the river. We will wait twenty minutes and then set off up the concrete road. I have kept a few oranges for myself as my water is getting low and is very warm.

Antonio never drank warm water from his bottle.

"Swill and spit, then suck on an orange," was his advice. "Warm water will give you stomach cramps."

As usual, he was probably right. When Pete and I first experienced the fierce Andalucian heat, we placed bottles of water in the freezer part of our fridge to make it icy-cold.

"Don't drink that!" Antonio shouted at me.

"Why ever not? It's delicious," I said, swigging the bottle, savouring the coolness of the near-frozen water.

"Because, English person, it will give you a sore throat!"

Of course I didn't believe him. Then two days later my throat closed up and throbbed for a week.

"Today," he announced, as we walked the goats over a hill, "I will take you to a well where the water is pure gold."

"Where is this magic water, Antonio?"

"Halfway to Barcelona."

It has always amazed us *guiris* (foreigners) how the Spanish can work out who is who, despite so many having the name Juan, Antonio or Maria. A man, for example, might go into a bar and say to the bartender, "Have you seen Juan in here this morning?"

Now, had someone shouted, "Is there anyone here by the name of Juan?" about thirty hands would have been raised. So how would the bartender know which Juan was was being looked for?

Well, it's simple. The chap asking the question was a painter and decorator, so it would follow that the Juan he was looking for would be Juan the 'paint'. We then have Antonio the 'goat', Pedro the 'taxi' or Maria the 'flower' (florist). Although this is logical, it then takes a twist. Antonio tried to explain.

"Who would Pepe *Rapido* (quick) be?" he asked me.

"Ah, that's easy, Antonio." I had put on my Sherlock Holmes hat, puffed at a pretend pipe and was getting into this Spanish nickname malarkey. "This chap would be wiry, quick and probably small."

"No, no, no. Pepe *Rapido* is big, fat and very, very slow!"

I was baffled.

"Look, Pedro the 'car'," Antonio explained, "is the chap that only rides his mule and Jose the 'laugh' is that miserable bastard up the road from me. Do you get it now?"

I didn't but nodded. The whole afternoon would be taken up with obscure nicknames and it was getting too hot for my feeble, fried brain to take in.

'Barcelona' was one of Antonio's pieces of land that he had seeded with grass for the goats to eat. He called them 'greens' and each had its own name. He phoned me one morning to tell me to walk my goats and to meet him at the long green.

"Which long green would that be?"

"The green, Diane! The green!"

"What bloody green, Antonio? You have about six!"

"Oh, right. Well, it's the one where that motorbike was parked last month."

And so the naming began. Motorbike green, ruin green, Diego's green, Dad's green and bucket green. (He once found a useful black bucket which had been slung in a ditch on the edge of the field).

After walking further afield to 'Valencia', (yet another green!), we finally arrived at the last, huge green of 'Barcelona'. I had, at that time, only visited 'Barcelona' on the tractor to see how the grass was growing.

This particular day was a goat-walk along narrow dusty tracks with neatly pruned olive groves on either side. Antonio's dogs were kept busy guarding the prize olives. By the time Antonio turned the herd off the track, dogs and humans were hot, cranky and thirsty. The goats had dashed to the shelter of a magnificent oak tree, with outstretched limbs, welcoming the exhausted goats into its shade.

"Hurry up, Diane," he said. "The goats are thirsty but you need to be the first to taste the gold. But first empty your water bottle for goodness sake!"

I staggered up towards him, reluctant to empty my precious water bottle. He snatched it out of my hand, unscrewed the lid and tipped the lukewarm contents onto the path.

"Here it is. The golden water!"

He pointed to a round brick well that was overgrown with wild honeysuckle and brambles.

"You mean this is it? This is the golden water? *Hombre*, please!"

There was little chance that I would ever drink from that well but I realised, right now, I had no choice.

Adding a length of string to the handle, he lowered my bottle into the well, prodded it down with a long stick and waited. Finally, he pulled the bottle up and took a swig. He wasn't being ungentlemanly, he just wanted to prove that the water wasn't poisonous.

"Drink the gold!"

I drank and, oh yes, it was pure gold. Coming from a cool mountain spring, the temperature was perfect. He quickly filled up both our bottles then bucketed water into a small nearby trough. The goats knew this water and ran to drink their fill.

"Now Diane, there are only a few people left in the *campo* who know about this well. Keep it to yourself."

I nodded, not daring to tell him that I'd probably never find it again with my useless sense of direction.

The alarm buzzed at 5.30 am. I rolled onto my back, my eyes still glued together.

"Pete, Pete," I whispered, digging my elbow into his back.

"What now?" he mumbled. "I'm asleep. Can't it wait 'til morning?"

"It is bloody morning. We have to move."

"Sod off," he said, burying his head deeper into his pillow.

Our dogs, Paz and Monty, entered the bedroom, farted, and then walked out again. I had one eye open now. I slowly swung my legs out of the bed and felt for my slippers.

Opening the front door to let the dogs out, the fresh morning air hit my face and my other eye shot open. Spring had arrived at last and babies were due over the next few days. Six had already arrived and we needed an early start in order to have everyone fed and milked.

The stables and pens needed cleaning before the next lot of arrivals. I prepared the horse and goat feed as Pete, now in his Wellingtons, checked the girls by torchlight through half-closed eyes.

I whistled to the boys and heard a distant whicker along with the sound of cantering hooves. The theme music from *Black Beauty* filled my head, and I smiled the first smile of the day.

I was born in 1954, at number 5, Sidney Cottages, St Mary's Cray, Kent. On that morning my sister, Sandra, and foster sister, Elizabeth, both aged ten, escaped from the bustling midwife and headed off to the local riding stables.

Sandra saddled up a pony named Black Beauty. 'Black' was the only bit of her name that carried any truth because the 'beauty' part had clearly skipped a generation. Elizabeth was on Bess. (I am amazed how they can both remember the horses names, sixty-odd years later, but now find their memories challenged when looking inside a fridge!)

They hacked around the country lanes close to our cottage. It occurred to my sister, while cantering on the grass verges, that she should perhaps pop home to see if 'the baby' had arrived. Dad, hearing the sound of hooves, dashed downstairs to meet her.

"You have a baby sister!" he told her.

She threw her reins to Liz and ran upstairs. Ignoring the midwife's tuts, Sandra came close and touched my hand and that's where it all began. I smelled horse. Outside, Beauty was getting impatient and began pawing the ground and snorting. I heard horse. From the moment of being a new-born, I was hooked.

Hardy and Beau arrived in a flourish of snorts and swirling hooves, snapping me out of my nostalgia.

"Brekky ready, old girl?" asked Hardy.

"Would that be our food you have there, in that bucket?" asked Beau, in his soft Dublin accent.

Checking them over by torchlight, to make sure no injuries had occurred overnight, I sniffed their necks and that wonderful, spicy perfume of horse refreshed me more than the first coffee of the day.

"Diane, hurry up. Alice is being a bloody cow!" Pete shouted from the milking shed.

I pondered at that remark. I thought better of shouting a witty reply at this hour of the day.

"On my way. I'll bring coffee."

After the winter storms, our large well had to be rebuilt. Before work could commence we needed a machine to clean it out. The machine was due any day now, but this is Spain. We were already on our fourth *manana*. We lived in hope that today would be the day that the 'man' would arrive to sort out the well, hence the early start.

We erected a temporary fence to keep the horses away and, on Antonio's advice, laid down black plastic to deter foxes from getting close and falling in. He also instructed Pete to pee around the plastic to keep the animals away. I'm not sure if Pete did but he often took the dogs that way for their last evening stroll.

Alice was pacified with an orange and a banana. Pete was pacified with coffee and toast. The day was racing ahead of us. Antonio had phoned to say that he was bringing his herd down to graze on our land, as three of his girls were in the early stages of labour.

Pete and I managed to grab a cupful of chicken soup, that I'd had simmering on the stove, before the afternoon shift began. At midday, Antonio had already arrived on our land and I took our girls out to meet him.

Pete set about scrubbing the pens, and preparing new ones for incoming babies. My young girl, Enya, had gone into labour and Antonio's goat, Rosa, was also just about ready to push when I reached him.

"I'll guard the well, Diane," he said. "Can you get these two sorted out?"

Rosa didn't need any assistance from me. Four grunts later and out dropped a huge boy. Enya, on the other hand, panted, pushed and was looking to me for help.

"Everything okay?" called Antonio.

"Yep, I've got the front legs, just pulling now."

With a huge grunt and a cry from Enya, and a steady pull from me, out popped a small, but perfectly-formed girl.

"Bravo," said Antonio, at my shoulder, still not trusting me to deliver my hundredth baby correctly.

Then we heard the splash.

"Shit, shit, a goat has fallen in!" shouted Antonio, as he raced to the well.

It was my young goat, Mandy. Heavily pregnant and not the sharpest tool in the shed, she had walked onto the black plastic and had slipped in.

"Get into the well, Antonio and save her!" I ordered him.

He was holding on to the bright yellow flexi-pipe that pumped the water up from the well, trying to make a grab for her horns. I was leaning over the side, trying to grab her horns too. I felt myself sliding into the well, which was about five metres deep. Antonio shouted at me to get back. I could see Mandy losing her strength while trying to keep afloat. Her head was getting lower in the water, her weight dragging her under.

"Antonio! Get that goat out NOW!"

He found a foothold inside the well, before pulling out his sling shot that was looped inside his belt. He quickly turned it into a lasso and threw the loop at Mandy's horns. His aim was true and he pulled tight. Holding the flexi-pipe with one hand, he steadily dragged Mandy to the side of the well.

It took all his strength to keep her head above the water and she was now in a state of panic. There was no time to run and find Pete. Phoning wouldn't work either as there is no signal in the sheds.

"Okay. Stay calm, Diane," Antonio said. "You need to hold her head above the water while I climb out. Three seconds, that's all it will take."

I lay down and hooked my feet over a tree root.

"Make it quick, Antonio."

Those few seconds felt like an eternity. She was so heavy. My feet immediately uncurled from my anchor and I edged towards the well. Mandy's head was going under the water.

A strong hand grabbed the rope from me.

"Okay, we have her. Help me pull her up."

We heaved her over the side of the well. My hands were shaking as I released the rope from her horns. Mandy shook herself dry, then walked away to the herd in search of her mother. She was badly shaken, as was I. She delivered a beautiful baby girl later that evening. All was well and the arrival of Daisy took her mind off the fact that she'd nearly drowned.

As for me, I couldn't get the picture out of my mind of seeing my sweet Mandy's head disappear under the water. The following day the machine came and cleaned the well. Work commenced and a fantastic new well house was built. I prayed this would be the last time we would have to rescue a goat from a well.

I shouldn't have held my breath on that one.

8

The Oven

At exactly 5 pm, Antonio phones.

"I'm going to pick the old girls up now from the lost garden. Are you close to climbing the *horno*?"

"Sniffy and Abuela are with me and we'll be starting up in a few minutes," I reply.

"Diane, those two cannot make that track. I told you to leave them at the garden. Are you mad?" His voice is getting louder.

"Antonio, I'll walk with them. There shouldn't be any traffic on the track. They will be safe."

I hope these are reassuring words. I am wrong.

"No, no, Diane! You need to be at the head of the herd."

I now have to hold the phone away from my ear as his voice has turned up to full volume.

"Don't worry," I say, knowing those two words will have him jumping up and down in frustration. "Don't worry. I have Chinni."

I quickly terminate the call.

Yes, I have Chinni. I expect her to hold the two herds together on this wide concrete track, a track that the sun has turned into an oven. It isn't only the heat which makes this part of the walk difficult. No matter what time of the year, it always gives us problems.

The first part is a very steep climb. Then, as it rounds a bend, the right hand side becomes dangerous. Although wonderful herbs are growing on that side, they disguise a cliff edge.

The other side is a rough grazing hill on which young trail-bike riders come to practice their dare-devil skills. Then there are the four-wheel drives that sometimes race down the *horno*, confident they are the only ones on the road, testing their nerves on a sharp bend.

For Chinni and me, the real problem is at the end of the road. It is a bend that has olive trees and Antonio's long green to distract them. I need the goats to turn right and then right again, onto a small track that leads down to the river.

I start them up the initial steep climb. I am fairly confident we won't meet a four-wheel drive. But a teenager on a trail-bike could make it tricky, or nasty, depending on...well, depending on me. I was reminded of that other time.

It had been a long hot day. We were bringing the goats back from the long trek to the *molino* where Antonio had done a few repair jobs on the sheds, before moving them there next month.

We had just rounded a bend and were on the long steep climb down the *horno*, when a trail-bike zoomed down from the hill and began weaving in and out of the goats. The teenager revved his machine every three seconds, scaring the goats witless.

"*Hombre*!" shouted Antonio. "Stop the bike for a few minutes."

The rider took no notice of Antonio's words or his hand signals to slow down. The red mist danced in front of my eyes. I needed Clint Eastwood, my often called upon alter ego, to take over. I stood in the middle of the road, smiled and beckoned the rider to 'make my day'. He revved his machine and I got my Magnum 44, sorry, my walking stick, into position.

"Diane, don't," called out Antonio, who was standing a few feet behind me.

Antonio had worked out what I was about to do. It was my stick versus the trail-bike's spokes. I ignored him and waited for the biker to make the first move. Would the punk have the courage? Apparently not. He pulled his bike over to the side of the track and turned his engine off.

I would like to think that the young biker saw *Dirty Harry* holding his Magnum by his side, munching on a hot dog. The thing I had forgotten, in all the excitement, was that Antonio also had an alter ego. In fact he had a few. Kwai Chang Caine when he Kung Fu'd in the *campo*, Indiana Jones when he swirled his sling shot and Crocodile Dundee for general *campo* emergencies.

I turned and smiled smugly at my friend, only to be met with an equally smug smile. Had he used the two-fingered hypnotic horn sign? Or did he pull out his ever-present hatchet from his belt? I didn't ask.

Clint came to my rescue again one dark evening in the Andalucian *campo*.

It was the evening of the World Cup final, Holland versus Spain. My goats were staying the night at the *molino*, Antonio's summer residence. He had prepared a makeshift corral for them.

"I don't want Alice getting into any fights with my girls," he said.

Antonio wanted to watch the match at the *molino* whilst Peter would watch it with friends at a bar in the local town. This was pre-arranged and Antonio mistakenly assumed I would be joining Pete in the bar.

"I'm not going into town dressed like this," I said, looking down at my filthy shorts and sweat stained T-shirt.

"You can't walk back Diane. It will be dark before you are halfway home. And you don't have the dogs. You don't have Monty to protect you."

That was true. I had left my dogs at Las Vicarias. Pete and I had scraped the money together to de-flea the lot. It was very expensive and it meant that we humans were on a diet of bread, cheese and tomatoes for a week. Antonio had, again, forgotten to buy the flea treatment for his dogs. Until he forked out for the tablets, I was keeping my dogs at home.

He was getting quite agitated now. He couldn't drive me home as his Land Rover was illegal, and he dare not risk driving on the main road at night.

"Stay here at my house and Pedro can pick you up later."

"No, no," I said, as I started to jog towards the river bed. "I'll be fine."

I needed to get a good pace going if I was to make it to the lost garden before dark. From there it was a straightforward track up to Antonio's sheds, then down the path to home. I crossed the river once then crossed it again. My feet hit every stepping stone, which was a first for me.

I could hear the sound of tooting car horns coming from the town. Spain must have scored a goal. There was one narrow cliff crossing ahead of me but, with no goats to tip me off the edge, I felt confident. Up and over I went, with no broken bones or grazed knees.

I stopped to catch my breath, then took off at a fast walk through the olive groves and reached the steep, concrete oven track. The light was fading fast. I pushed on but as I got to the bottom, God turned off the lights.

"Bugger," I said out loud.

I don't get easily spooked at night. There is that moment when you can hear the day time creatures settling down and the night time creatures waking up. We do have wild boar but they seldom come close to the goat paths and are quite shy.

My only concern was scorpions. My left boot had a tiny hole in the sole and I hoped one didn't scuttle out in front of me. I had one more cliff path to climb but I convinced myself that, if I literally hugged the cliff, I would stay on a straight line to the lost garden. Despite getting my hands bloodied, by getting them tangled up in a bramble bush, I finally made it.

I squinted ahead, trying to make out the top pathway. I saw lights or, to be precise, the glow from cigarettes. People were sitting by the side of the path, smoking. It could only be robbers. Everyone else was in the town watching the football match.

It was a perfect opportunity to rob a *finca*, or break into Antonio's sheds and steal his solar panel and tools. What to do? I was tired, hungry and frankly felt a little vulnerable. In the *campo*, no one would hear me scream.

"Get a grip, Diane," I muttered to myself. "Deal with it."

It was time for my old friend to take over. I dragged my straw cowboy hat from my rucksack and bent it back into shape. As soon as I placed it on my head, it happened. I became the 'man with no name'.

Feeling for my rifle (discreetly hidden under my poncho), I practiced reciting the line, 'my mule gets the notion you're laughing at him'. I walked slowly along the path, spitting a few times (I'm not quite sure why). Practically on top of the smokers, I moved my poncho aside and lifted my Winchester (stick), to shoulder height.

"Evening, gentlemen," I mumbled, wishing I had a cheroot wedged in the side of my mouth.

No reply. I squinted in their direction, the lights still glowing at me until… Ah, wait a second. The lights were green, not red. Glow worms. Clint disappeared and I went back to being the idiot in the *campo*. The phone rang.

"Are you back yet?" Antonio asked

"Nearly at your sheds," I replied, trying to sound jolly.

"Good, good. So you didn't bump into the ghost of old Diego's father by the second bridge then?" He began to giggle. "Oh, and we won the World Cup."

The first part of the *horno* is a very steep climb. I try to keep pace with Chinni as she takes the herd up. I am not sure if she is trying to tire the goats out or escaping this heat trap as fast as possible. The bend in the road is coming up and she will soon be out of sight. I need all the goats bunched up together. I also have to keep an eye on Sniffy and the Abuela's progress.

El horno (the oven) and the second bridge.

"Hold them, Chinni, hold them."

She stops immediately and turns round. I put my hand up in a 'Stop' sign. She understands and sways her horns at the young machos who are trying to pass her. They stop and half-heartedly nibble the herbs at the side of the road. All the girls are in a tight bunch with Sniffy and Abuela in the rear. I jog up and stand beside Chinni.

"Okay, Chin, take them off. Nice and steady."

I watch as she leads them along the last stretch of the road and I check the goats as they pass me. All the babies are doing fine and keeping tight with their mums. Sniffy and the Abuela are starting to fall back again. Sniffy barely makes three paces before she has to stop and rest. I look at Chinni who is now close to the olives and the turn-off to the river. I will her to turn around and look at me. She does.

"Take them to the river, Chinni," I say, waving my arm to the right.

The goats are hot and thirsty, and don't need much persuading to make the right-hand turn. Chinni remains standing by the olives until the last goat walks down to the river. Only then does she follow. At the same time, I turn back to the old girls to see how I can help them walk up this punishing track. It takes nearly thirty minutes to reach the river turn off.

Sniffy is physically finished. She is too big and too heavy for me to put her on my shoulders so the Abuela takes over. She quietly walks next to her old friend and nudges her. Sniffy picks up her invisible Zimmer frame and, with true grit and determination, reaches the river and drinks.

This will be our last resting place. Chin takes some time to eat and I just take some time. We are on the home run to the *molino*.

9

Monty and Paz

The old olive grove, where the goats are now resting, is owned by Antonio's father. It has been left open to nature, without being tended to for many years, and is a place the family like to visit for picnics. No chemicals have ever been sprayed on it. Full of wild flowers, with olive trees giving perfect shade, it is ideal for humans and animals.

I help Sniffy and the Abuela to a vacant tree, where they slowly ease themselves down and promptly fall asleep. Chinni is quietly weaving her way up-river to prevent any goat prematurely leaving the grove. I feel it's time to give my feet another soaking in the river to cool them down.

Removing my boots and rather ripe socks, I station myself on a rock in the middle of the river. Chinni and I have a clear view of the herd and each other. I dip my straw hat into the river. In movies I have seen many a cowboy do this, after riding through a hot and dusty canyon and rounding up cattle. They dip their stetsons into a stream and the water cascades down their faces.

Filled with cool river water, I place mine back on my head. Unfortunately, my straw hat buckles under the weight of the water and the overall effect is not that of an American cowboy, more like

Worzel Gummidge the scarecrow after a rain storm. My head is cooling down at last and I close my eyes. I can feel the sand and river cleaning and soothing my feet.

Alas, my peace is shattered. Alice has spied my unguarded rucksack on the river bank and, even though I have placed my smelly socks over it, the pong doesn't deter her. She is determined, at all costs, to get inside and steal any food.

Not wanting to disturb the sleeping herd by chucking a stone at her, I leave my rock and swish my way back to the river bank.

"You bloody witch, Alice!" I snarl. "If Paz was here you would be in big trouble. Now bugger off!"

She doesn't bugger off. All that's left in my arsenal is 'the stare.' I twist my neck and then lock on to her eyes. She does the same. Who will be the first to blink? My eyes begin to sting as sweat drips into them. Alice has no such problem. In fact, she takes one step towards me.

Then a miracle arrives in the shape of a horse fly. It lands on her ear. She shakes her head, turns, farts loudly in my direction and returns to her sleeping daughters.

I miss the dogs. Alice is no match for Paz and the *campo* is no match for Monty. Both guard me with their lives.

I have never been good at home security. I thought I had little of value to interest thieves. Unless, of course, they were keen book readers, looking for a rare first edition, which I did not own. So there was no need to lock my front or back doors.

My home town of Swanage, in Dorset, was a sleepy little coastal town that only really came to life in July and August and again at New Year's Eve. Friends popped in and out, day and night, regardless of whether I was at home or not. Perhaps they had a cake to be shared, wanted to borrow a book, or simply needed a quiet place to get away from teenagers. On Sunday mornings I was often woken with a shout from downstairs.

"Tea's made!"

That would be my friend, Philip. He would drop in at 7 am, boil the kettle, make tea and toast and read the Sunday papers. He would leave them strewn over the dining table.

This all came as a bit of a shock to a boy brought up in the city of Birmingham when Peter and I married. The nightly 'lock-up' was a normal routine for him. He even locked my car door.

Why bother? I mean, who in his right mind would steal an old red Panda with hit-and-miss brakes? Unless one knew the subtle technique of stopping the old girl, any unsuspecting thief would find himself embedded firmly in the wall at the end of our street.

I couldn't break Peter's habit of locking the doors at night or when we left the house. So I placed a couple of spare door keys in a pot and normal service was resumed. In time Peter got used to staggering downstairs in the morning and being welcomed with a mug of tea from someone who wasn't his wife.

Moving to Las Vicarias, I became a little more security conscious. When driving into town we locked our front door and, even though our windows had no glass, iron bars prevented anyone from climbing in. Our possessions consisted mainly of photographs, important paperwork, Peter's guitars, my saddles, and boxes of books. The guitars and saddles, we believed, were the only items to interest thieves. We were sadly mistaken.

Daughter, Felicity, was visiting. A trip into town was needed to buy cleaning materials and plastic wine glasses. Fliss is as accident prone as her mother and can't be trusted with anything made from glass.

Purchasing bleach, anti-grease spray or loo cleaner is not easy. The local supermarket has shelves full of stuff but with no clear pictures on the sides of the bottles to explain their use. There can be up to six Brits in a line, staring at the different coloured bottles. Armed with dictionaries and with spectacles perched on the ends of noses, they pray for divine intervention. Mind you, it is quite a good conversation opener.

"Is this washing machine liquid or fabric conditioner?"

"What the hell is *Agua fuerte*?" It says 'strong water' in the dictionary."

Not one of us, in the early days, had the courage to ask an assistant. We just paid for it and prayed it was right.

Upon our return, I unpacked the magic cleaners while Pete went into House Two to prepare the horse feed.

"Diane! Come here quickly!" he shouted.

I stood next to him trying to see what the fuss was about, hoping it wasn't a huge snake or a scorpion he had encountered.

"It's gone! It's all gone!"

"What's all gone, for crying out loud?"

"The tools have! All of our bloody tools are gone!"

My eyes began to focus on the bare walls and empty work bench. Drills, grinder, and four boxes of other tools that had yet to be unpacked, were all gone. I phoned Antonio.

"It's no use phoning the police," he said, "they won't help."

"What do we do then?"

"Buy fencing and gates. I'll meet you at the co-operative in half an hour."

Over the next few days, Pete and Antonio banged in posts, attached very expensive chain link fence and hung double gates.

"When you go out, lock the gates," Antonio said. "Trust no one."

I was close to tears.

"I didn't think anyone would steal our tools. The guitars and saddles were locked up inside the house."

"Are you mad, woman? This lot would steal the coat from your back if they could. Just keep *everything* locked away."

Felicity arrived and, although saddened that we had been robbed, she was most impressed with the new gates and fencing.

Word got around that our tools had been stolen. We were not surprised, one hot afternoon, to see Rafael thundering up to our gates in his four-wheel drive. He leapt out.

"*Hola*, good people!" he shouted.

"How nice of him to come and check we are okay," said Peter as he opened the gates.

Personally I thought he'd come to ogle at my beautiful daughter. But I smiled and nodded.

"Come in Rafael. Come and have a beer," said Peter.

"It is a terrible thing, Pedro, for a man to have his tools stolen," said Rafael, shaking his head solemnly.

He then opened up the truck's back door and out jumped a huge gangly puppy.

"Oh, bring your dog in too. It's hot in the truck."

We sat outside drinking cold beer and Rafael regaled us with stories of local houses being broken into. The huge black-and-tan pup sniffed around for a while then fell asleep at my feet.

"Right, I must be off. Lots of jobs to do," said Rafael as he leapt up and jogged towards his truck.

"Don't forget your pup," I called.

"I brought the dog for you, woman. This fence won't keep the robbers out. But he will. He is my gift to your family in this tragic time."

He then jumped into the truck and drove away, leaving me spitting out the swirling dust he left behind.

"He says that the dog is his present to us."

The three of us stared at the pup, who in turn stared back at us, wagging his tail.

Monty

"Let's call him Monty," said Fliss, who was now on the floor playing with the pup.

I like to be organized. I like to be prepared. I was not

accustomed to this Spanish way of sudden surprises. Unexpected visits. Puppies being thrust upon me!

With no puppy food in the house and no bed prepared, what were we to do? The only thing left was to open a bottle of wine which was being saved for supper. Two glasses later, I had the courage to phone Rafael.

"Yes, speak," said Rafael.

"The pup, how old is he and what is he?"

"Three months old. Mastin. Good parents." He cut the call.

We made a quick supper and fed Monty pasta and chicken. It was time for bed. Pete dragged an old horse blanket into the kitchen.

"He can sleep on that tonight."

Monty, however, had other ideas. He followed us into the bedroom, curled up on the floor next to me and fell fast asleep.

Felicty flew back to England with a promise of another visit at Christmas.

On hearing that we had acquired a puppy, Antonio came down, bringing his new young Mastin, Luna, with him. Both were the same age and they bonded and became puppyhood sweethearts.

"Walk him with your little ones, Diane. He needs to know that his job is to protect you and them."

"Are you sure he won't hurt them? He is so big."

"He is a Mastin, Diane. Trust him."

Monty was perfect with the young kids. He also loved Carmen and the two formed a very special friendship. While kids played on the rock face, Carmen, Chinni and Monty walked quietly around our olive grove.

I did some basic training with Monty, teaching him to stay, to come back, and to lie down. I wasn't sure what else one could teach a Mastin.

The time came to call the kids down from the hill behind the house. It had been getting more and more difficult to extract the little darlings from their playground. After nearly an hour of climbing, shooing and swearing, the little buggers still wouldn't come down. As if somebody had rubbed a magic lamp, Antonio appeared.

"I see you have a problem," he said.

"They won't come back down. I don't know what to do."

Antonio squinted in the direction of the wayward kids and whistled. All four came down immediately. They ran past me and into the corral with Carmen, Chinni and Monty hot on their heels.

"You need a water dog," he said.

"I have Monty. I don't need a water dog for these few goats."

"Yes, you do. By the time I have trained one for you, your herd will be a lot bigger."

He was right of course. I had no control over these few. How would I cope with twenty or more?

"Chivvi will give birth in a couple of weeks and you can have one of her pups."

Chivvi is one of Antonio's sweet young dogs. She is a mixture of Turko, Poodle and something else. She is a wonderful dog on the hills, bringing goats back down purely on Antonio's hand signals. No rushing, no nipping, just gentle pushing. Antonio's method was to talk to her.

"Chivvi, there are two goats up in that bush. Bring them down please."

Off she would run and gently but firmly usher the goats back down to the herd.

Antonio believes that all animals want to work and communicate with humans. The problem is that humans do not know how to communicate with animals. Also, each animal should be treated as an individual. His training methods are always the same but he allows each dog to develop its own personality and quirks.

"Antonio, you have just spoken to Chivvi in Spanish, without hand signals or a change of tone."

He gave me the 'idiot woman' look.

"You learn Spanish by listening to me, yes?"

"Yes, but I am a human, not a dog."

"*Dios*, I already speak dog! *They* have to learn *my* language!"

"Okay, of course. Aren't I the silly one?"

Two weeks later, he phoned to tell me that Chivvi had given birth.

"Two girls. Come up and see."

We found Antonio fussing over Chivvi and stroking what looked like two mice.

"One of these will be yours," he beamed, like a proud father.

"They look beautiful," I said.

"No, they don't, Diane. They look like mice. But in a few weeks they will be beautiful and you can choose which one you want to be yours."

Felicity arrived the week before Christmas, bringing gravy granules and sage and onion stuffing.

"Flippin' heck mother, Monty is huge now!" she said cuddling the gangly youth.

He was still sleeping by my bedside at night, squeezing his body into the gap between bed and wall. He was my shadow.

Winter had arrived early in the valley. In the past, we had spent Christmas day in shorts and T-shirts. But this winter was very different. A thick frost covered the land in the early morning and on Antonio's instructions, Felicity and I boiled kettles to pour hot water into the goat's water buckets to prevent them from freezing over.

In the evenings, they were put into a small stable with a nice warm bed and the kids snuggled into Carmen's woolly coat. It was bloody cold. Luckily for us, Fliss had also brought over a couple of electric blankets. Generator on, blankets turned up to number three, pure bliss.

"Bring Fliss up to choose which puppy you are having," said Antonio, phoning early one evening. "Hot chocolate would be nice."

Armed with a flask and mugs, the three of us trooped up to the sheds. Not waiting for me to pour the drinks, Antonio dashed into the dog-pen and carried out two fluffy black pups. With a big smile, he gave both to Felicity.

"Choose one, Fliss," he said.

She cuddled them both, before looking to me for help.

"Mum, I can't decide. Suppose I choose the wrong one?"

She handed me both the puppies. One was covered in wood ash from Antonio's makeshift fire in the big shed.

"Ah yes," said Antonio. "That one crawls into the ash at night. Chivvi likes the other one best."

I held the scruffy one close to me and examined her. She had four white paws and a very curly coat. She looked up at me and it was a done deal.

"This is the one, Antonio."

"You're sure?"

"Yes, I'm sure," I said, holding her face to mine.

Before any of us English had time to decide what we would call her, Antonio took her from me and held her up.

"I name you Paz," he said, turning to his English audience. "It's Christmas time."

Paz means peace.

We drank hot chocolate and cuddled the pups for an hour. Then, just as we were about to leave, Antonio beckoned me over to a pen.

"See these four kids? They have all been rejected by their mums."

"Oh, how sad for them."

"They are yours."

"What, all of them? They really are all mine?"

"Now you have Paz, we will have to build your herd up fast," he said with a huge grin.

A few weeks later I was allowed to bring Paz home. I bundled her up inside my jacket shielding her against the biting wind that was whipping around the valley. Pete had the wood-burner blazing, the goats were locked in, the horses were fed and stew was bubbling on the cooker.

My only worry now was Monty, would he accept this pup? She was tiny. Would he be as gentle with her as he was with the kids? I walked inside the house, the heat blasting my face. It was pure heaven. Monty was sprawled next to the fire. I placed Paz next to him.

"Monty, meet Paz. Paz, meet Monty."

Pete shoved a mug of hot chocolate into my hands and we stood back to watch. Paz was mesmerized by the flames flickering behind the wood-burner's glass door. Monty sniffed her, came and sniffed me then went back to the pup and gently lay down next to her.

That night I felt a cold nose on my face.

"What's the matter, Monts?" I asked.

He turned and walked out of the bedroom. I followed him as he led me to the pup who was having a little cry. All became clear. I opened the front door and was met with a blast of cold air.

Paz waddled out, had a pee and waddled back to the fire. Monty waited for her to settle down before laying his huge body next to hers. It was the beginning of a life-time of friendship.

10

Little and Large

Chinni stands up, which is a signal to me that it's time to move the herd on. I want to walk beside her on this last leg of the trek but have decided that this is her moment, not mine.

Every night when the goats are having their last minute feeding on the hills, Chinni waits for the command from me to 'take them home, Chinni, take them home'. She then leads them back to the sheds. I thought it right to always give the same command.

"Okay, are we all ready? Take them home, Chinni, take them home."

With a flick of her horns, the herd stands and we all move off.

The river is wide and shallow, allowing the goats to meander along either side, eating the lush grass growing on the river banks. In twenty minutes we will be at the *molino* and my girls can have a rest before we head back to Las Vicarias.

The birds are out in force now, swooping and gobbling up insects. Bee-eaters are diving in and out of their nests, tunneled into the sides of the river banks. How do they judge it? How do they blast into their nests at full speed, brake, feed the babies, turn around, then zoom at full throttle back out again? It's all a mystery to me.

Terrapins are having a chin wag on the rocks and plop into the water as we walk past their houses buried in the banks. On seeing the approaching herd, one almost hears them say, as they slip into the river, "Oh bugger! Them there goats are back! Dive! Dive! *Dive!*"

As a young girl, I loved all the animal programmes. *Mr Ed*, the famous talking horse, *Animal Magic* and *Tales of the River Bank*. The wonderful Johnny Morris engaged children by giving the animals voices. Apparently this anthropomorphic thing became frowned upon and his programmes were closed down.

I couldn't understand this as Disney continues to make a fortune by giving animals a voice, not to mention insurance companies. When my children were little I gave voices to the animals and creatures we encountered walking in the country park. We would see cats sitting on walls, ants, worms, birds and rabbits. The girls loved it.

At dusk we would sit outside and listen to the birds settling down in the trees.

"Oi, Mavis, move over! And who made that smell?"

They learned to watch and listen to all animals and, of course, in time, they too gave voices to the creatures. A drama could be made when watching snails or a colony of ants steadily crawling up a wall, giving an account of their day. It was fun.

Antonio sometimes did the same. On one occasion his goats were being naughty, climbing high on the hills and he had to send Chivvi up, again and again, to bring them down. He lost his patience.

"Will you bunch of shits come down now and behave yourselves! Next time I'll send Pirri up after you, and you won't like that will you?"

The goats all turned to stare in astonishment at the shouting Antonio. Seldom did their friend raise a voice at them.

"Can you hear what they are saying, Diane? Listen, listen."

Not trusting that I could translate his 'goat' Spanish into my rubbish Spanish, he translated for me.

"Hark at him. Milk prices must be down!"

He often chatted to ants.

We had seeded our field and Antonio came down to inspect it. I brought him a cup of hot chocolate and found him on his hands and knees in conversation with an ant.

"No, no," he said, lifting a seed from the back of an ant. "You can't rob Diane's seeds."

I watched as he continued to lift seeds from a colony of marching ants.

"I don't care how many babies you have to feed, these seeds are for the goats, not you."

"Oh, I see," I said, nodding in a sympathetic way. "They have families to feed."

Antonio turned his head very slowly and stared at me.

"Are you mad, Diane? Ants are robbing, lying bastards."

He jumped onto his tractor shaking his head and leaving me, as usual, blinking rapidly, my mouth open and utterly speechless.

I have always had the great fortune to have had dogs, cats and horses in my life. But this was the first time I have actually worked with them.

Seeing Antonio and his dogs communicate with each other left me in awe. I worried that I might not achieve such a level of trust and respect with my little dog, Paz.

Antonio was moving to the mill for the summer and he wanted to take Paz with him.

"Look, Diane, she needs to learn from her mother and I will teach her how to be a good hill dog."

"But she might not want to come back home to me," I said, feeling the panic rising in my voice.

"Of course she will come back. She just needs to be with me this summer."

"Okay, but not today. Let's wait until you have settled in at the *molino* and I will walk her over to you."

I thought that was a good compromise and a sensible plan. Antonio sighed. He knew he had a fight on his hands.

It was Paz who eventually made the decision. A few weeks later Antonio walked his goats downriver and we met up late in the afternoon. Pete joined us, bringing three cans of cold *sin*-alcohol beer. We sat on the bridge and sipped.

"Thought any more about bringing Paz over to the *molino,* Diane?" he said, keeping his eyes on Peter.

"Yes, yes. I thought next week we could drive her over," I replied with a big smile.

Peter, aware that Antonio was looking for some support, thought it best to focus on an interestingly-shaped stone.

"Right, well, must be off then as it's getting late. Bye."

He walked off without a backward glance, his goats and dogs following him in a perfect line. Paz watched them go.

Paz

"Come on Paz, let's go home," I said, as Pete started to 'shoo' our girls downriver. Paz came and stood in front of me.

"Diane, she's asking to go," Peter said quietly.

"It's okay Paz," I said, my voice starting to wobble. "Go. Go find Antonio."

She turned and scampered upriver. Peter phoned Antonio.

"Paz is on her way."

She stayed at the *molino* for nearly three months. I visited her once a week.

"She is going to be a first-class hill dog Diane. Come and watch this."

Half a dozen goats had climbed up the very steep hill opposite the mill. Antonio walked Paz and her mother, Chivvi, to the bottom. He placed one hand on Chivvi's collar, and with the other he signaled to Paz.

"Bring them down, Paz. *Arriba, arriba,*" he said, his arm sweeping round to give her the signal to go.

Paz took off without looking at her mother.

"Watch this, Diane. Watch."

Paz climbed above the goats and ran at them. As they scooted down the hill, Paz stopped and looked around to check she hadn't missed anyone.

"And that," said Antonio, "is a good working dog,"

He motioned her to come down. She ran down and straight past Antonio and into my arms. She was no longer a pup. Her body had turned into firm muscle.

She still had a few more weeks of training before Antonio returned to his winter sheds. She watched me drive away and didn't try to follow the car.

Had I lost her?

Peter helped Antonio to move all of his equipment back to the winter sheds at the top of our track. It was nearly dark by the time he got home.

"Antonio's on his way. I've set the goat food up for him. You go and collect Paz."

Leaving Pete to check our goats were settled down for the night, I started up the track. The lights were on in the sheds, so Antonio was back. In the distance I could make out the silhouettes of dogs, sitting in his top paddock, waiting to be fed. My stomach began to churn.

Suppose she didn't want to leave Antonio? Maybe she was happier with him and his bigger herd. I made my mind up. If she wanted to stay, I would be happy for her.

And then something bumped into my legs.

"Hello, mum!"

She had met me halfway down the track, making for home.

Monty had gone from being a gangly teenager to a big strong adult. Everyone respected him, most of all Antonio. He knew that this young dog was dangerous out in the *campo*.

"You are being rather dramatic," I said, when he instructed me to clip Monty on the lead having spotted his cousin walking towards the herd.

"Diane, clip him on now. He is young and full of himself."

By the time I had pulled out the lead, which was buried deep in my rucksack, the cousin had arrived. Antonio's dogs barked at him and he shooed them away.

"Get away with you," he said, as he waved his stick in their general direction.

Monty had walked forward.

"You too!" his cousin shouted, waving his stick at Monty.

"Shit!" muttered Antonio. "Don't move, Paco!"

I ran to Monty and clipped on his lead. Monty let out a deep growl.

"Stand still, Paco," instructed Antonio. "Trust me."

Antonio took Monty's lead from me.

"Just let him sniff you and drop your stick," said Antonio.

The cousin stood still, his eyes widening. Antonio let Monty sniff his terrified cousin who was by now staring straight ahead, not moving and uttering not a word. Monty sniffed his feet, legs and then his balls. His long nose gently lifted Paco's 'equipment', held the position for a few seconds, let them drop and then sat down.

"You're safe now. Come and have a smoke."

Antonio handed the lead back to me.

"Good boy, Monts," I said scratching behind his ears.

"Bloody idiot waved a stick at me!" Monty said to me, in his Prince Charles voice. "Doesn't he know who I am?"

It had been raining for three days. Good rain, rain that soaked into the ground and soaked into your skin. Antonio had walked his herd upriver but I decided to stay local, grazing the goats in the lost garden.

It had been a cold and drizzly afternoon and the goat paths on the hills were muddy and unstable. I had left Monty and Paz at home because hunters were around and Monty does not like hunters. Paz needed an afternoon off, free to enjoy the warmth of the fire.

I could manage a day without them and everyone needs a day off. It was an hour before dusk. I was cold and tired so I turned the girls and told Chinni to take them home. They took the high hill path while Carmen the sheep and I walked on the bottom track.

We were approaching Antonio's sheds. I looked up the hill to see the herd picking up speed. This was unusual as Chinni always kept them at a steady pace. Maybe they were as pissed off with the weather as I was. Patty, Cassie and our disabled girls, Mikki, Gerona and Ruby, were lagging behind.

Then I saw them. Four hunting dogs were standing above the five goats. Times were hard and the four must have been let loose to fend for themselves. They were hungry and my girls looked tasty. I understood and felt sad for the dogs, but not sad enough to offer my goats on a plate.

"Clear off, you bastards!" I shouted.

I quickly began to climb up the hill but my boots couldn't get a purchase. The bank just fell away. The dogs split up and circled the goats. I had to make a split-second decision. I phoned Peter.

"Let Monty out, NOW!"

I heard Pete open our gate.

"Go find Mum, Monty. Go, go!"

He then spoke to me.

"He's on his way!"

I cut the call, not wanting to lose time explaining the drama that was unfolding.

"Monty, HELP!" I shouted to the sky.

In those few moments of Pete opening the gates, I knew I had put my dog, my friend, in danger. Four, big, hungry hunting dogs could hurt Monty badly if they turned to fight. But four, big, hungry hunting dogs were about to attack my best 'milkers' and darling special-needs girls.

I dragged myself up the hill, slipping and cursing. If the goats ran now, the dogs would attack. The pack had spread out, waiting for one of the goats to make the first move.

"I'm coming girls!" I shouted.

I saw the dogs brace themselves for the attack. They stood still, eyes locked onto my special-needs goats that had leg problems and hoof deformities. Goats unable to run. I felt helpless and the tears started to roll. Telling myself to move faster, I climbed higher, digging my toes and finger tips into the mud, shouting and swearing at the dogs.

The pack suddenly started to move backwards. Was this a new tactic? Were they getting ready to leap? All four dogs changed their body language. I looked to my left and there he was, standing on top of a huge rock. Monty. I crawled up some more and was now on the same path as the girls. Patty picked up speed and the rest followed. They knew Monty was there to guard them.

I looked down and saw that Carmen had run to Antonio's sheds, waiting to pick up the special-needs girls. I was the rear-guard. We passed Monty but I didn't acknowledge him. His eyes were locked onto the hunting dogs. His presence, his energy, his duty as our guardian, was enough to stop the pack in their tracks.

I was nearly home when Monty caught up with me.

"Thank you Monty," I said, taking his head in my hands and kissing him.

His tail wagged, and we turned for home.

Paz and Monty are a perfect team. At lunch time, when I take my herd out and I munch cheese and tomato sandwiches, Paz is on alert and Monty snoozes. A car may appear on a distant track. Paz will leap into action to wake Monty.

"Oi, Monty. There's a car on the road," she whispers into the ear of the sleeping Mastin.

Monty will immediately get up and watch the vehicle. It could be a farmer or it could be a hunter. Paz, meanwhile, keeps one eye on the goats, ready for the command from Monty to move the herd. I, of course, eat an orange and leave all the major decisions to the dogs.

"Is everything okay, Paz?" I ask, not sure if I should pack up my rucksack and tighten my boot laces. I am normally met with a rather condescending stare from my little friend.

"All under control, Mum. You carry on eating and don't forget to leave me the crusts."

Only when Monty is satisfied that any danger has passed, will he go back to his pitch and snooze. Paz relaxes and comes back to sit next to me, waiting for the promised crusts of bread.

At the end of a long day and having taken care of me and the goats, Paz and Monty take time to let off steam. As soon as the goats are safely across the last bridge and walking along the river banks, the dogs dash onto the sand. They roll, scratching their backs, legs waving in the air. If only I could do the same.

Their day is at an end while I am still trying to fathom what Pete and I could have for dinner from a depleted larder. I watched 'Little and Large' play-fighting until Monty espied a terrapin slowly making its way to the river.

These are my observations of the events that followed and I

thank the late, great Johnny Morris, for showing me how to interpret animals' conversations.

"Leave that bloody terrapin alone, Monty," says Paz, scratching her back in the sand.

Monty stares at the terrapin in wonder.

"Oh look, Paz, this is a splendid little thing."

Paz gets up, shaking the sand from her fur and walks over to her friend. Both dogs lower their heads and stare at the terrapin slowly making its way towards the river. Monty blocks its chosen path.

"Monty, get out of the bloody way," says Paz in her little cockney voice. "They like the water. They're semi-aquatic."

"Well, this little one is far too young to be without its mummy. I'll just help it back up the bank."

"I wouldn't do that if I were you," advises Paz, shaking her head as the big Mastin gently picks up the terrapin in his mouth.

"Gy?" Monty asks.

"What you say?"

"I ged gy?"

"Oh! You said why! Why shouldn't you pick up a terrapin?"

"Ges, gaz, gy?"

I move a little closer. Paz is sitting in front of Monty who is gently holding the creature in his mouth and nodding his head. Not in agreement with his little friend, rather trying to sooth the terrapin. By now it's shooting all four of its legs in and out of its shell in terror.

"They get scared, Monty. And being in your jaws could give it an 'eart attack."

"Gon't ge gilly, gaz!"

"I'm not being silly. It's just advice. You can take it or leave it. But when a terrapin gets scared it'll pee. And the way you're holding it, you'll cop a gob-full."

"Gaa, gat's gisgusting!" splutters Monty.

He drops the dazed terrapin and runs to the river.

"Ungrateful wretch," he gags, between large gulps of water.

Paz looks at me and to this day I swear she winked.

11

Pensioners

Antonio is standing on the river bank waiting to welcome the goats back to their summer home. Chinni lifts her head high and quickens her pace. She has safely brought his herd home, her job is now done.

I watch her as she walks up the bank. She looks neither at Antonio nor the freshly filled water trough but heads straight for the shade of the huge eucalyptus tree that stands in the middle of the corral. It's time to rest.

"All present and correct, sir," I say to Antonio, giving him a salute.

"Where are the old girls?" he asks, squinting downriver.

"They're coming. Chinni was amazing, she took care of everyone."

We both turn to look at the hero of the day. Her eyes are closed as she rests her head against the tree.

"Diane, she's a ghost. She's a dead goat walking."

He says these words quietly. They are not meant to hurt, only to prepare me for losing her.

"She is my Chinni, Antonio, and she is not finished yet."

"*Sí*, amiga. Chinni is one in a billion."

He quickly separates the mums that have babies waiting for them. The babies were brought to the *molino* in his Land Rover. He ushers me into the store room.

"There's a beer in the cupboard for you," he says, "and a banana."

The last time I visited the mill it was full of sand and mud. The storms had brought the river over the corral and into the sheds. Antonio had to hire a digger to clear up the mess. Peter had spent a couple of days helping to fence the corral and to place the water tanks higher up. These needed additional piping to fill the drinking troughs.

Today, Antonio has swept and organized the store room. Roosting perches for his chickens are in place. Little ladders lead up to nesting boxes which he has nailed to the wall. An old door is now resting on some breeze-blocks serving as a make-shift dining table. There is also a seventies-type cupboard with four doors and two drawers, all painted green. His mother, a few years ago, had given him two cupboards, one for here and one for his winter sheds.

I open one of the doors to locate the beer and fruit. It is clean and neat. Medicines and syringes in one corner, water, beer and fruit in the other. The drawers housed a hammer, screws and nails, wire, rope and a car-jack, all carefully set out.

"How long is it going to stay this tidy?" I call out to Antonio, who is busy helping the babies feed from their mums.

"Have you no faith, woman?"

"If I'm honest with you, Antonio, no. Remember Juanito?"

"Ah yes. Juanito, the bastard."

It was a cold February morning. We had finished milking and Pete had left the farm to deliver the milk to the local cheese-making factory. I was preparing a soup for lunch when the phone rang.

"I need a hand," whispered Antonio.

"Why are you whispering?"

"I don't want him to hear."

"Who are you talking about?" I whispered back.

"Juanito. And today I'm going to murder him."

Juanito is a rat.

Antonio believes that all creatures can live together in harmony. Provided everyone respected the other's personal space, all would be well. Paquita, a long, black snake, lives mostly in his feed store. Rats and mice are quickly and efficiently gobbled up. There was no need for rat poison. Occasionally Paquita steals the chickens' eggs but Antonio is philosophical about that. Everyone needs a change of diet.

However, Juanito the rat, has managed to evade the snake's jaws for over a year. He entertains Antonio in the mornings by swinging on the overhead light cables, like a trapeze artist, before sitting by the dogs, waiting for left-over tit-bits to be shared out. All was harmonious until that February morning.

I turned off the soup and jogged up the track to the sheds.

"What's happened?"

Antonio motioned me to whisper.

"The bastard has bitten through the solar cable and I had to milk by torchlight."

"Righto. So where is he?" I whispered

"He's in the cupboard," he said, with a manic smile. "I have a plan."

"And what, may I ask, is your plan?"

"This rope." He waved a long piece of plaited bailing-twine. "This rope will be tied to the drawer handle. You pull the rope, he jumps out and I'll bash him with my stick."

"Interesting plan. But it won't work."

"Yes, it will," he said, carefully tying the rope round the drawer handle."

"It won't work!" My whispering went up an octave.

"Yes, it will. Stop arguing and get into position."

"Antonio, it won't work because..." He shut me up with a wave of his hand and handed me the rope.

He held his stick shoulder high and began mouthing to me.

"Uno..."

"But Antonio…"

"Dos…"

"But if I pull…"

"Tres!" He signalled to pull.

I pulled and the cupboard started to fall on top of us. Antonio swished his stick up and down like a man possessed. We both managed to leap out of the way just as the cupboard bounced on the floor, covering us in a cloud of dust and cobwebs. No sign of Juanito who had escaped his execution.

The contents of the cupboard were scattered all over the floor of the milking parlour. Nails, screws, bits of 'things-that-may-come-in-useful-one-day', medicines, and just plain rubbish. It was a mess.

I stared at Antonio while removing dusty cobwebs from my face and hair. As usual he hadn't listened to me. I knew the drawers were stuffed with heavy hammers and other tools. They were full to bursting.

I continued to stare at the idiot, who by now had lost his psycho-killer face and thought a boyish grin might smooth the situation.

"I needed to clean that cupboard out anyway. I couldn't find a thing before. I'll get a sack and we can put all the rubbish in it."

Juanito was forgotten and I left without uttering a word.

Antonio is back outside, waiting on the river bank for Sniffy and the Abuela to appear. I stand next to him, sipping my cool beer.

"They'll be fine," I reassure him. "Just very tired. Do you remember the film, *The Incredible Journey*?"

"Yes, yes. The old dog made it home. What was his name?"

"Bodger. You cried watching that film. I know you cried."

"No, I didn't."

"You cried, Antonio!"

"I had a noodle in my throat," he says, climbing down the river bank. "I'm going to meet them."

These two old ladies have a special place in his heart. He once let them down and he never forgave himself.

The Abuela's real name was Juana. She had been one of his best milkers and her offspring were also good producers. She was old, and he had renamed her *la Abuela* (grandmother) as a sign of his respect and gratitude for all the milk she had provided over the years.

When it was mating time he separated her and a few other old girls into a large pen, bringing them fresh olive cuttings to eat. They had served him well and deserved a good retirement. Old goat herders that came, either to visit or collect manure for their allotments, would comment on the old goats munching in the pens.

"Are those for the meat wagon, Rubio (Blondie)?"

"Yes, the man is coming tomorrow," Antonio would reply.

He couldn't be seen to be a soft Andalucian goat herder and so he played the game.

The Abuela had come into season and the bucks started to take an interest. At night he would put her into a secure dog pen. Normally she would be kept in the day pen which, although strong, a randy buck could and would jump over.

It had been a long day for Antonio and a long night. He had a few goats giving birth, and a few rejected babies to feed. By midnight, he was knackered. He put all his chickens on their perches for the night and then realised one was missing. He finally found her roosting in an olive tree. With his wind-up torch in his mouth he climbed up the tree, grabbed her and took her back to the sheds. With the threat of a downpour he couldn't leave her out all night. He was exhausted.

He locked up and jumped into his tractor, heading for home, food and bed, but had forgotten to move the Abuela. The following morning he found Bruce Lee with her. Bruce had jumped the pen and indulged in a night of romance without being interrupted by other jealous bucks. Antonio clung to the hope that the old girl would abort early, because of her age, and all would be well. She didn't. She went full term.

Peter and I had just climbed into bed when the phone rang at 11 pm. I held the phone outside the front door for a better signal. It could only be Antonio at this time of night.

"It's the Abuela, I have killed her," he said.

"We're on our way up," I said, not understanding what he meant.

We climbed out of our clean pajamas and back into our dirty work clothes before staggering up the track, still half asleep. The valley was silent except for the loud groans of a goat.

"What's happened?" I asked.

"She can't pass the babies. They're dead now and I can't turn them and get them out. You will have to do it, Diane."

Antonio needed my small hands to get the dead babies into a position for him to be able to make the final pull. I went in and double-checked for any reflex from the stuck baby. Not a thing. This gave me options. I could hook onto, or into, anything that would help bring the baby's head forwards and into position. The Abuela was moaning, too exhausted to cry out.

"Hurry up, Diane, we will lose her."

"I've done it! Head and legs are in position."

I kept one finger on the head, as Antonio felt for the legs and then pulled. A perfectly formed but very large boy now lay on the concrete floor. Antonio bumped up the Abuela's tummy which pushed the second baby into position. I went in again. This one's head was turned backwards. It took a little longer to get it into the right position but Antonio was already holding one leg, ready for my signal.

"Okay, now pull!"

It was a beautiful baby girl. We laid her next to her brother. The Abuela was too far gone to even sniff her dead children. She collapsed and moaned no more.

"This is my fault. I have killed her and her babies."

He sat down on his upturned beer crate, his head in his hands. He was overtired and one mistake had cost him the life of his dear old goat.

"Shut up," I said. "Get the drench."

Peter had run back down to our house to collect hot water. He was now mixing it with molasses. I gently syringed the thick nourishing liquid into her mouth.

"Get the Oxytocin and draw five millilitres."

This was the first time Antonio allowed me to give orders and make decisions. He looked at me for only a second before drawing the drug into a syringe. The old girl was too weak to push out the afterbirth and I didn't want to take any more risks with her. A retained placenta kills. The drug will do the work for her, it said so on the packet.

I had never used the drug before, and neither had Antonio, but the vet had recommended it. Antonio, who doesn't trust vets, had not bothered to open up the box and read the small print. I had read that dogs having multiple births were given this. There was nothing to lose so I took a gamble.

The gamble paid off. We sat on beer crates covered in goo, blood, sweat and tears. Two dead babies lay next to us.

"I've brought up some alfalfa," said Peter very quietly.

Antonio jumped up and into action. He prepared a clean pen for her and then, with Pete's help, gently lifted the tired old girl onto a clean warm bed. He placed the alfalfa and warm water next to her. We left at around 1 am, and at 7 am my phone rang.

"She is up and eating. In forty-eight hours we'll know if she'll survive."

He sounded calm. He sounded hopeful.

Two days later she was out, walking with the herd.

Other than La Mocha (hornless goat), I can't remember the original name of Sniffy, or even if she had one. Sniffy sniffed. It was as if she had a permanently runny nose. I called her Sniffy and Antonio called her Niffy.

She was old and quite severely crippled. A year earlier, Sniffy's back leg had been twisted and dislocated when it was caught in another goat's horns. The leg couldn't be repaired, but she found a way of walking by swinging her back leg out and propelling herself forward.

She too had become pregnant at the same time as the Abuela. Bruce Lee had been a very busy boy. She gave birth, with no problems, to a beautiful girl.

The rains had come, swelling the river. Antonio had taken the herd across the narrow bridge to graze on his hills. He left Sniffy and her little girl locked up in the pens. She needed more time to recover. Should he need to quickly bring the herd back down from the hill, she wouldn't be able to keep up.

I didn't want to chance the weather. The skies looked threatening so I kept my girls on our land, close to home. Sure enough, at 5 pm, the heavens opened and the girls and I made a fast dash to our sheds. In the distance, I heard a faint rumble of thunder.

"Pete," I shouted, above the din of the rain pelting down on the shed's tin roof, "lock the horses in the back paddock."

"Already done. They are safe and the electric fence is on," Pete shouted from House Two. "I'm just making up the goat feed."

While Peter was sorting out the buckets, I grabbed the binoculars, threw a dry jacket over my head and rushed back into the field, searching the hills for Antonio. I sighed with relief when I saw goats running for the bridge. Antonio had, at the most, fifteen minutes to get them all across safely before the river came over the top. I waited an hour before telephoning him.

"Are you okay?"

"All okay, except Sniffy and her baby got out of the pen and are now stuck on the other side of the river."

"Oh no! What can we do?"

"Nothing Diane. We can do nothing until the river goes down a bit. She will be okay, don't worry."

But I did worry. The rain fell hard all night. It was cold, wet and windy. Sniffy was alone with her baby and we couldn't rescue her.

A day later the rain eased. I walked to Antonio's high cliff paddock with my binoculars. I scanned the hills, but there was no sign of Sniffy.

"We have to find her, Antonio."

"Maybe I can get across tomorrow but today I have to take the goats to the other hill to graze. There is nothing we can do but wait until tomorrow."

I took my girls out early and grazed them in our olive grove. It was blowing a gale. By 4.30 pm I'd had enough, and so had the girls. Peter had prepared their dinner and was dishing it out into their troughs. The goats heard the dinner gong and ran for their supper and the warmth of the stables.

In our house, the wood burner was blazing and a stew was bubbling away on the stove. I made a hot chocolate and Pete added a capful of brandy to it. We groaned with relief and ecstasy as we hauled off our Wellington boots and stuck our smelly-socked feet close to the fire.

Paz and Monty accepted the pong as we accepted their farts. I closed my eyes to savour this end-of-the-day moment. It didn't last. My thoughts soon turned to Sniffy. I couldn't enjoy this warmth and comfort while she was out there somewhere with a young baby. I reached for my Wellingtons.

"I have to go to the bridge, Peter, to see if there is any trace of her."

"Not on your own you're not," he said, wearily reaching for his boots.

The light was fading fast by the time we reached the bridge.

"We can just get across," said Peter. "Follow my steps."

We carefully pigeon-stepped along the narrow homemade bridge. On the other side, I scanned the ground looking for any fresh tracks or droppings but there was nothing. Climbing up the steep bank into the old olive grove, I called her name. The wind was too loud to hear any reply.

"Maybe she made it to the old ruin," said Peter.

We picked up speed and crossed the *arroyo* via huge stepping stones, then jogged to a small roofless ruin on Antonio's land. There she lay, with her baby tightly snuggled into her. She was freezing cold and breathing hard. I phoned Antonio, having to shout above the wind.

"Come and get them. They are safe but Sniffy is in a bad way," I told him.

I lay down next to the old girl, trying to warm her. Antonio arrived and knelt down next to Sniffy.

"She won't make it, Diane. I can't carry her across the bridge and up the track. I'll take the baby back to the sheds."

The rain began to fall.

"Diane, we have to go," said Peter. "This rain is coming down hard, we have to go now."

Antonio lifted the baby over his shoulders and made off at a fast pace to the bridge. Peter pushed me out of the ruin and we jogged to catch up with Antonio. It was scary crossing the bridge as the light was nearly gone and the river was rising.

I was silent walking up the steep track from the river to Antonio's sheds. He was chatting away to the little girl curled around his neck. The sheds were warm and the goats were settled down for the night.

"She can sleep in the big pen tonight," he said. "It's nice and warm." He tried to sound upbeat, sensing my downbeat mood.

My mind was racing. This was wrong. Sniffy had protected her little girl, got her to a safe place and kept her warm. We don't leave anyone behind.

"Peter, get the rope from the top shed. Antonio, we're going back."

"Diane, we can't get her across the bridge, it's impossible," he said.

"We're not going that way," I said meeting his eyes. "Start the tractor."

"Her leg won't take the journey. She will be in terrible pain and she will get drenched in the tractor bucket." Antonio's eyes held mine.

Peter arrived with the rope. He wasn't sure how this confrontation between his wife and Antonio would end. He thought it wise to keep quiet and study the rope in detail.

There is a limit to how much Antonio can be ordered about by an English woman. We held the stare. Who would blink first? It was Antonio. To save face, he now took over.

"Get in," he shouted, revving the tractor engine. "We'll take a good run at the river so hold tight."

Pete and I braced ourselves as he plunged the tractor down the bank and into the fast current of the river. I closed my eyes and Pete swore, his back slamming into the small passenger seat. We raced across his cousin's olive grove and onto Antonio's land.

I still had my eyes tightly shut as he turned the tractor and reversed to the ruin. He lowered the tractor bucket keeping the engine running. The three of us jumped out. The rain was heavier now and there was no time to lose. Sniffy didn't raise her head when we rushed into the ruin but did when Antonio spoke.

"Come on, girl, we're going home."

Peter and Antonio lifted her into the bucket. It took all of her willpower to stay upright. Antonio weaved the rope around her and pulled it as tight as he dared without cutting off all her circulation.

"I don't know how she will hold up when we drive across the river and up the steep track," he said.

"It's okay, I'm sitting in the bucket with her," I said.

Peter thought this was madness but kept quiet as adrenaline was running high. The wind was picking up again and so was the rain. I climbed in and Antonio raised the bucket. I was scared but Sniffy wasn't. She was going home to her baby.

The tractor took off and I gripped the bucket's metal sides, pushing my shoulder into Sniffy. Peter opened up the tractor window.

"River coming up, hold tight," he shouted.

Antonio took the tractor into the river at a good speed. The water lapped into the bucket as we climbed the bank on the other side, but we made it. Now for the steep climb up the track to the sheds.

I pushed my back into Sniffy's body to keep her steady. At last we arrived at the sheds and Antonio reversed up to the doors. Pete hauled me out of the bucket and Antonio quickly untied the ropes.

Pete helped him carry her into the pen where her baby was sleeping and the two men carefully laid the old girl next to her daughter.

Sniffy bent her head and began to lick the little girl. Water, alfalfa and a dose of molasses was given to her and Antonio stacked up his makeshift fire to keep her warm. There was nothing more we could do.

The following day, after milking, I visited Antonio. There she was, old Sniffy, up and feeding her baby.

"I've named the girl Miracle," he said, giving me a huge smile.

12

Mothers

Antonio walks Sniffy and the Abuela slowly back to the mill.

"I'll feed them in the back room away from the others," he says, gently guiding them through the herd.

"Okay. It's time now for me to get back to Las Vicarias."

Chinni is already up and heading towards the river.

"Come on girls," I call. "Let's go home."

"Which way are you going?"

"I'm keeping to the river. My girls will wade in, no problem."

My girls rise and follow Chinni. I turn to wave at my friend but he is deep in conversation with his two old girls.

We head to the canyon. To get there we have to cross the river three times. With no prize olive groves to protect, Chinni and I can relax and enjoy this part of the walk. The girls seem happy to have left Antonio's herd behind. I watch as they quickly seek out friends and family to walk with and catch up on the day's gossip.

All is going well until the mosquitos attack. I should have sprayed myself with the magic anti-mosquito liquid before I left the *molino*. Now I have to dive into my rucksack to find it and that means Alice may hear me rummaging.

I thrust my arm deep inside and waggle my hand around.

Germoline, orange, splints, bandages, haven't got a clue (boiled egg?), spray.

Alice lurks in the cane grass, watching. When her best friend Pepita died I tried to take Pepita's place, loving her unconditionally. It hasn't always been easy. Alice dashes out of the cane just as my hand clamps around the spray.

"I want that orange!" she cries.

"One moment Alice, if you please," I mutter.

"I want that orange and I want it now!"

She stands in front of me, her eyes staring into mine.

"Okay, okay. I'll give you a bloody orange."

I let go of the spray and begin rummaging again.

Germoline, splints, bandages.

"Now!" she screams.

"Wait a second will you? I'm trying my best!"

"Give it to me!" she yells, as I remove it from the rucksack.

I hold up the battered fruit and watch as Alice tips her head back and clamps her jaws, squirting juice everywhere. My hand quickly dives back inside the rucksack.

Pulling out the spray I run into the cane grass, squirting anti-mozzie all over myself. I haul the rucksack onto my shoulders out of reach of Alice.

To enjoy a handful of peanuts, when out walking, I have to wait until Alice is a speck in the distance. The bag is carefully removed from the rucksack and opened very, very quietly. After pouring a handful out I only have a few seconds to chew and swallow before she is sprinting towards me.

"Peanuts! Give! Now!"

Antonio has far more patience with her.

"Alice, I have your packed lunch ready for you," he says in a calm tone.

"Oh Antonio," she purrs, sitting next to him, "you are so kind."

From his rucksack he pulls out a paper bag full of old bananas, bread and oranges. Lunch finished, she makes a big fuss of him while he smirks at me.

"You just have to know how to handle her, Diane."

Self-preservation, at all costs. That's Alice.

It was near the end of summer. Antonio was still at the mill, leaving the valley empty for me and the girls to wander through freely. A welcome breeze in the late afternoon meant I could take the girls high up onto Antonio's hill and let them graze on fresh herbs.

I had lost track of time but Chinni hadn't. She started to move the girls downhill to the second bridge. Her plan, it seemed, was to walk along the river bed before losing the daylight. Monty and Paz chose a path that was safe for me to walk and together we headed for the river. Goats and dogs drank from the clear water and I checked that all the goats were present and correct. They were not.

"Where's Alice?" I asked the girls.

"Don't know and don't care," was the general response.

It wasn't just Alice who was missing. Her daughters and the idiots, Cassy and Daisy, could not be found. I reached for my phone.

"Antonio, Alice and about six others are missing. I think they are up on the second hill. I'm in the river bed. What should I do?"

Antonio was used to these phone calls from me.

"Don't worry, Diane, Alice will come down and catch you up."

"But it will be dark soon and she will be scared."

"Alice, scared? Don't be silly and stop panicking."

Paz was scanning the hill.

"Let's go home, Paz, she'll probably meet us there."

Paz was not convinced.

We jogged to catch up with the herd. Chinni, determined to get all the goats back home before it was dark, kept up a steady pace. As the last goat entered the stables, we lost the light. Peter went outside to call for Alice while I grabbed a mug of tea. There was no sign of her.

"That's it. I'm off to find her. She's probably stuck on the hill, too scared to come down in the dark," I said, grabbing my wind-up torch.

It was slow going, winding as I jogged. Eventually I crossed the little bridge and headed for the second hill.

"Alice!" I screamed into the darkness.

After twenty minutes I had lost my bearings and just about lost my voice. The phone rang.

"You are in the middle of nowhere and calling Alice, *sí*?"

"Yes, I am and I can't find her."

"Well, you won't because she is with me."

"WHAT?"

Apparently I still had enough voice left to shout at Antonio.

"She turned up with her daughters and a couple of others shortly after you phoned. I tried to phone you but the signal was bad."

"But why did she come to you and not come home?"

"*Dios* woman, it's Alice. She knew she couldn't make it back before dark so she made a dash to the mill. She took care of her daughters and the others."

"Alice? Are you kidding? She ran for safety and the others just followed her!"

Paz and I got up very early the next morning and walked to the mill. We found Alice and her cohorts standing together in a corral. I could see the light from Antonio's torch in the sheds. I decided not to say hello. I couldn't face the smirk. I stared at Alice.

"Home, now. I have Paz and she is very pissed off."

Paz took over.

"Quick…march! You bleedin' 'orrible lot!"

Alice led the way, her head held high, followed by Cassy, Daisy and her four daughters. I smiled for it was a wonderful sight to see the four siblings so close together. And it was Elizabeth who made that all happen.

Alice has her own set of maternity rules. Give birth, feed, put kid to bed, job done for the day. The rest of the mothers allowed the babies to use them as trampolines and when they tired of jumping up and down on their tired mother's backs they would run around the corral, exploring and playing with the other kids.

Alice put her babies to bed on her pallet and expected them to stay there until the next feed. She wandered around the herd, mocking the other mothers who were running from paddock to paddock trying to locate a lost child. Her idea of motherly love was giving her baby a whole pallet to itself.

Alice claimed two pallets in the best stable and she protected them, and her babies, in her own unique way. If another goat came close to these posh beds, she would give a menacing stare followed by, "Bugger off, you common thing or a horn will be up your nose!"

It always worked. Her babies grew up feeling not only special, but entitled to respect. Her first born was a big, cuddly hornless girl who bore no resemblance to her mother at all. We named her Patty and Alice doted on her. Patty was the perfect kid, obeying her mother and enjoying the little time Alice gave to playing with her.

Her next baby was the beautiful Willow. She had the same colouring as her mother, with the buds of horns to come. Alice shoved Patty off the family pallet and replaced her with the new baby. Patty was upset and couldn't work out why her mother had thrown her out of the family home. Pepita took over, and invited the rejected girl to join her family.

For a year, Willow enjoyed being treated like a princess. She always had the best olive tree to shade under, best pallet to sleep on and best position at the feed trough. All was well until Alice gave birth to the twins. We named them Elizabeth and Jennifer. Elizabeth was big and strong, with the buds of horns, while Jennifer was a little smaller and hornless.

Willow was thrown out and the twins took her place. Unlike the gentle Patty, Willow rebelled. She changed from a wonderfully behaved teenage girl into one that used the 'f' word at every opportunity. I couldn't control her, Paz couldn't control her and even Antonio and his dogs couldn't control her.

She raided olive groves, defying the dogs sent to bring her out by climbing up a tree. Every goat that got in her way ended up in a fight. She wouldn't make friends or turn to Auntie Pepita for comfort. Willow's heart was broken. Maybe by acting tough she thought her mother would notice her but Alice only had eyes for the twins.

When the twins were old enough to walk out with the herd, Willow waited for every opportunity to bash them with her horns. Elizabeth and Jennifer ran to their mother for protection and Alice chased Willow away. There was nothing I could do for her. Elizabeth grew a beautiful pair of horns and started to stand up to the attacks but Jennifer was scared and kept close to Alice for protection.

More than a year later, history repeated itself. Alice gave birth to Eileen. The twins were chucked out and Eileen replaced them. Jennifer cried and cried. She tried to get close to her mother but was chased away.

Elizabeth took care of her twin. She protected her from Willow and comforted her when Alice ignored her. Then something strange happened.

I was sitting under a eucalyptus tree at the lost garden, sharing my lunch with Alice. Little Eileen slept between us. Elizabeth and Jennifer were sitting at a safe distance away from their mother, watching Eileen enjoying their mother's attentions.

Elizabeth got up and walked over to the far side of the river where Willow was sleeping. Jennifer trotted close behind. She must have thought her sister mad, walking into Willow's territory. Paz was immediately on the alert.

"Trouble brewing, mum," she said.

"Sit tight, Paz. Let's just see what happens."

Elizabeth slowly sat down in front of Willow. Jennifer sat down behind her sister, trying to make herself invisible. I couldn't make out what on earth was going on. These sworn enemies looked like they were having some sort of family meeting. Five minutes went by then all three stood up and walked towards me.

I felt Paz tense up again. Most days she had to dash between Willow and another goat to break up a fight. I put my hand on her collar. The three rejected daughters came to the edge of the invisible circle that Alice marked out around herself, allowing no goat inside. The three took one step inside and sat down. I phoned Antonio to tell him the drama that was unfolding.

"They want their mother back, it's that simple. If Alice doesn't make eye contact with them, all will be well," he assured me.

It was time to move the goats up onto the hill before heading home. Paz and I slowly stood up. Eileen woke from her nap and bounced onto her mum. Alice stood up, shaking the little girl off her back and walked towards the hill, not looking at her three other daughters. I called the herd to get moving and Paz rounded up all the stragglers on the other side of the river.

Elizabeth, Jennifer and Willow followed their mother with Eileen running in between them. That night Pete and I went into the goat shed for the final check before bedtime. The royal pallets were full, Alice and her four daughters lay together chewing the cud, content.

I would like to think that Alice had realised that her daughters needed her love. But in truth she had lost her best friend, Pepita who always protected her. So perhaps there was safety in numbers. Alice. Self-preservation.

Antonio had a batch of new babies. Our friends, Julie and Andy, were visiting so, while Pete and her husband played guitars, we walked up the track to his sheds to indulge in kid cuddling.

"What's the matter with that little one?" asked Julie, pointing to a tiny sleeping kid.

"It's dying," said Antonio.

Julie looked at me, eyes wide.

"You have to take her, Diane," she said.

Antonio worked out the conversation.

"She won't make it, Diane. You don't need another baby to look after. She will be dead in twenty four hours, trust me."

End of conversation. We 'cooed' and cuddled for another twenty minutes. On leaving, we named the little dying baby Julia, as everyone needs a name and to be recognized as a living being, even if only for a short time. The following day I popped up to see how little Julia was doing. I knew Julie would phone later to ask after her.

"Still alive, Diane. I've given her a dose of antibiotics but it won't work."

"Can't I take her home with me please, Antonio?"

"No, she will die and you will cry."

Again, end of conversation. He was right of course. How many babies had we cuddled all night long, giving hours of care and, just when we thought we had saved them, they died in our arms.

I already had little Mariposa sleeping in a box next to our bed as she was too small to sleep in the baby crèche. Taking on another special-needs goat would be too much.

I decided not to visit Antonio for a few days. I would wait until I heard that little Julia had passed on to the goat heaven in the sky. The phone rang.

"Can you bring up the hoof trimmers? I can't find mine."

On entering the shed I avoided looking into what I assumed would be Julia's empty pen.

"She has a fifty per cent chance of survival, so you can take her," said Antonio, rolling a cigarette.

"What?"

"Julia. She is in there," he said, nodding to her pen.

The little girl was up and waddling around.

"She won't drink from a bottle so find her a good easy goat to feed her."

"Gerona. She would be the best one," I said.

"Okay, but don't forget how to protect her. Put your back facing Gerona's head and gently lift Julia on. Gerona may try and bite and that will put Julia off drinking."

Antonio had given me Gerona after her mother had given birth to four and he was overrun with extra kids needing milk. Gerona is a beautiful tri-coloured girl but although we handled her from a baby, she was not the most friendly of goats. Humans were not her thing. She kept herself to herself, not bothering anyone and no one bothered her. She was the ideal goat for Julia, as just one touch of her teat got the milk flowing.

I snuggled Julia under my coat and trotted back down to the farm. Peter quickly put a small pen together in the corner of the milking shed. While he took over cuddling duty I went into the other sheds, calling for Gerona. She looked up from her pallet. A goat of few words she stared at me, dead-eyed.

"Gerona dear, I need your help with a sick baby. Thank you."

Gerona continued to stare at me for a few minutes and then slowly stood up.

"Well done, Gerona, I knew you would help. It won't take long and then you'll be back in your bed."

She stopped and looked at me. It was quite obvious that my jolly chummy tone did not impress her and she thought me quite mad. Peter tied her up and we placed Julia by her teats. She drank both sides and Gerona didn't even flinch. We placed the baby back into her pen and gave Gerona some extra alfalfa to eat, as a thank you for being so quiet and gentle.

"Let's have a beer while she's eating," said Peter.

After finishing our second beer, we ambled back into the warm milking shed. Gerona was fast asleep next to Julia's pen. We crept back out. The following morning we tied Gerona up, put Julia on her teat and stood back to watch. Gerona stood stock still, allowing the baby to drink from both sides and didn't once turn to bite or nudge her.

I put Julia back into her pen and Pete untied Gerona. She walked back to the place where she had slept, right next to Julia, sat down and chewed the cud. Gerona only left this pitch when we went out walking in the *campo*. On our return she waited by the stable door, to be let in next to her adopted daughter. Gerona was in love.

Julia thrived and although she still had a strange waddling walk, it wasn't long before she was strong enough to come out with the herd. Gerona never left her side. Two years later, Julia gave birth. Antonio assured me that she would be fine but I had my doubts.

Except for her rolling gait, she was fit and healthy, but still I worried. It was a long labour and she was crying, so I phoned Antonio. By the time he had walked down to our stables, Julia was in agony, and I couldn't move the baby because my fingers were just not strong enough.

"The head is too big," said Antonio, examining her. "The baby is dead."

"So what's the bloody plan, Antonio?"

My nerves were frayed by the sound of Julia's cries.

"Pedro, hold Julia's head. Diane, go inside and hold the baby's leg. I'll move the head forward."

Julia was now on the floor screaming. Antonio managed to move the head forward and down while I held on to a tiny hoof. We were ready to pull. All this time Gerona was standing by the door, watching.

"Okay, pull, Diane, slowly but firmly," said Antonio.

A few moments later a very large dead kid was placed on the floor next to Julia who had now gone into shock. I needed to get vitamins and warm molasses inside her.

"Stand back everyone," said Antonio.

He had watched Gerona out of the corner of his eye and knew she was the best chance for Julia's recovery. As we moved away, Gerona ran in. She went down on her knees and licked and nuzzled her adopted daughter.

Julia slowly stood up and immediately Gerona stood in front of her, lifting her hind leg for Julia to suckle. A mother is always a mother, no matter how old a kid is. She will always give comfort, warmth and love.

Except Alice.

13

Antonio Tells a Story

Tying my boots onto my rucksack I walk into the warm, clear flowing river. The goats also dip their hooves and slowly paddle along the side of the bank, munching cane and bracken. Peace and tranquility. That is, until the phone rings.

"How this country gets anything done is a bloody mystery to me," says Peter, his irritated voice blasting into my ear. "I mean, how many bits of identification do I need to produce to confirm that we own our olive trees?"

The rant continues for a good five minutes. I hold the phone away from my ear and watch the bee-eaters swoop along the river banks, catching insects hovering above the goats. When the rant stops I quickly tune back in.

"Oh, bugger. I hope you have a cold beer to hand," I say, trying to sound sympathetic.

"Yes, just opened a tin. How are you doing?"

"I'm fine. Look, deep breaths. This is Spain and we are English. It's tricky."

I ring off and continue my slow sloshing downriver.

We try to be in town by 11 am to drop our milk off at the cheese factory. We then go to a bar that has wi-fi, grab a coffee and, if we are feeling rich, a slice of toast. At this time of the day there are normally some expats who are in need of comfort, tissues, advice or a drink.

By 11.30 am, many of these poor souls have spent the morning in banks, builder's yards, electricity offices or the post office. In a state of shock, they sit nursing a beverage. You can usually tell which office they have done battle with by the drink that is being cradled in front of them. Julie had a glass of white wine. Our eyes met.

"Electricity office," she whispered.

"Water board," said Dave, downing a shot of Anis.

"It's because we're English," said Nick, who had spent an hour at a builder's yard and was now on his second beer. "The Spanish wouldn't put up with the runaround we get."

I related these tales of woe to Antonio.

"Diane, we have the same problems. The trouble with you English is that you take it personally."

If anything goes wrong over a weekend in a small Spanish town, one is completely buggered. To find a plumber or an electrician on a Saturday morning is nigh on impossible.

Some of us are lucky enough to have a good Spanish neighbour who has a cousin that knows a chap, who, at a price, may help us with our boiler, electrics or blocked loo. But it will not be until next Tuesday.

Dropping off our milk at the cheese factory at weekends is a problem. Nobody at the factory wants to drive to the industrial estate to open the doors for us. They turn off their phones, hoping their colleagues will answer our calls.

When we have exhausted all the telephone numbers of owners and employees, we phone Antonio. Most times he has room in his chiller tank to take our weekend milk.

One Saturday, after spending half an hour calling for a door opener, I made the call to Antonio.

"Yes, that's fine, I have room but I seem to have a problem with the tank. I turned it on and it went *phst blerr.*"

"What do you mean *phst blerr?*"

"That's the sound it made, *phst blerr.* But it's okay, I will see my cousin and get him to look at it. He has fixed it before."

We arrived at his garage, poured the milk into his tank and left him to it.

The following day I made my way up to his sheds to check if the tank had been fixed. I also wanted to ask him to take our milk again, to save on the wasted phone calls.

"Did you get the tank fixed?"

"Yes, eventually," he said, pulling up two beer crates and motioning me to sit.

"What happened?"

And so Antonio's story began…

After you left, Rafael turned up, as his wife had kicked him out so that she could clean the house. He came with me to my cousin's house. My cousin's wife said that he wouldn't be back from his work in Jerez until 10 pm, but I could try Jose, who lives up by the school. He is a good electrician. So we drove there and found the house. I knocked on the door and his wife answered looking very angry. I asked for Jose, explaining that my cooler tank needed fixing pronto and she started shouting at me!

"No, he can't fix your tank as he's in Ronda hospital. The idiot went off on horseback with his brother this morning to help round up some cows. A bull got out and stuck its horn into his leg." Barely drawing breath, she continued. "It's my nephew's communion today, and I can't go because I have to travel down to f- g Ronda hospital to sit all night with that stupid idiot!"

I wanted to ask if the horse was okay, but thought better of it.

Rafael bravely asked if she knew of any other electrician that may help.

"Yes, you could try Pablo," she said, "but I don't have his number. So ring old Pedro. He may have it."

She wrote down old Pedro's number on a tiny piece of paper. I told Rafael to read it out, as I dialed. He didn't have his reading glasses with him so he had to hold the paper at arm's-length trying to read it. After the third go, I managed to get through.

"No, I don't have his number,' Pedro said. 'But Paco the cow will have it."

"What's his number?" I asked, trying to find a spare piece of paper to write it on.

"Oh no, Paco doesn't believe in mobile telephones. You will have to go round to his shed. But be quick as by now he will be on his third bottle of beer."

Well, time was running out as the milk was still sitting in the tank and needed to be cooled right away. So I phoned the driver of the milk lorry and asked him to come and pick up my milk today, two days earlier then arranged, explaining my problem.

"*Hombre*, sorry," he said. "I'm in Malaga but the young lad has the other lorry in Campillos, about half an hour away from you. He may have room."

"Great," I said. "Give me his mobile number."

"Ah, right. I'll text you his number, but he was on the piss last night so he may be sleeping off a hangover. Why not give Pedro the goat a ring? He may have some room in his tank?"

I phoned Pedro the goat but he didn't have room, and he was waiting for the hangover-lad to empty his tank. I phoned the piss-head.

"Get to Olvera now and empty my tank!" I shouted down the phone.

"Ok, ok, *hombre. Tranquillo*! (calm)" the little shit said.

By now we had arrived at the garage of Paco the cow. I explained that we needed the telephone number of Pablo, the electrician.

"Hang on, hang on, I do have it here somewhere," he said. "Help yourself to a drink while I go look for it."

Rafael grabbed a mug and filled it to the top with beer. I walked up and down for about ten minutes until Paco staggered back into the garage, waving a piece of paper at me.

"I said I had it! Now, *Rubio* (blondie), come and have a beer, you look really hacked off."

"No, I'm off. Are you coming, Rafael?"

"No, I'll stay here and chat for a while. I'll see you later."

I could see he was settled in for a session.

Antonio's voice trailed off as he rolled another cigarette. I waited for the next part of the story. This ought to have been titled, 'The Repair' but his train of thought seemed to have drifted so I nudged him along.

"So what was the problem with the tank?" I asked.

"The tank?"

"Yes, the bloody tank! What was the bloody problem?"

"Oh, there was no problem with the tank. It was the plug. It just needed a new fuse."

When the sun starts to dip in the late afternoon, the goats settle down to eat the herbs on the sides of the hills. This is the perfect time for two tired goatherders to sit, eat some fruit, and relax. This is also the hour when Antonio tells his stories and for me to learn Spanish. I use the word 'Spanish' in the loosest possible sense, for Antonio speaks 'Olvera Andaluz', the local dialect.

All expats make an effort to learn Spanish before embarking on their new life abroad. CDs are bought to be played during the car journey to work. Lesson One is played for the first twenty minutes. Not to strain our brains too much the CD is changed for Queen's Greatest Hits or, if suffering from a hangover, a Chopin Piano Concerto.

On one of the trips to Spain, searching for our dream home, we marvelled how far we had come when managing to order a meal. However, reality soon kicked in when the final big move happened and we had to order an oven or tiles.

Before entering a shop, we practiced the opening sentence for half an hour over coffee. But the answers left us red-faced and fumbling for our dictionary.

As the months progressed and our Spanish hadn't, drink came into play. I'm not sure if it loosens the brain or removes inhibitions, but somehow understanding the local accent became much easier. I had my own technique.

Antonio would rattle out, at machine-gun speed, the previous night's episode of *Red Eagle*, a brilliant television series about medieval Spain, with a hero who was a mixture of Robin Hood and Bruce Lee. He would recall every scene in detail. I would switch off, open my mouth like a goldfish and relax. It seemed to work. The words flowed and I grasped seventy per cent of them.

My favourite stories were about Antonio's family and life in the *campo* when he was a child, remembering the goatherders calling to each other across the hills. How mothers would mimic the same call in the evening by standing on the doorsteps of their houses and scream out a child's name when the evening meal was ready. Mothers still do this. English neighbours, clasp their ears to block out the Andaluz screech of 'Maria!' being shouted in unison at 8 pm.

"Did I tell you about the time when I was called up to do my time in the Army?"

He passed me some bread and an orange. I settled down, broke some bread and hoped I could keep up as he began…

An Army truck came to the town and half a dozen of us were picked up. It stopped at Pruna and Algodonales and a few other villages. We got down to the Cadiz camp and were shown to our barracks to unpack. We were all hungry. We'd had breakfast very early and had eaten the packed lunches our mums had made ages ago. And it was 8 pm now. A sergeant came into the hut.

"Grub up, boys," he said. "Follow me to the big tent."

We couldn't believe our eyes when we saw all the food on the table.

Big rolls full of meat, plates of cheese and fruit.

"Eat up lads," said the sergeant, who had a big moustache and a huge neck. "Then turn in as you have a big day tomorrow."

"We ate and ate, and agreed that the warnings that our fathers and big brothers had given us (that every sergeant was horrible) were just plain lies.

The following day it was still very dark when the sergeant came into the hut.

"Up, and get those beds made, quick and sharp!" he said in a very loud voice.

We all looked at each other in horror as none of us had ever made a bed before. Our mothers always did it. How hard could it be? We did our best and it looked okay. Ten minutes later the sergeant came back in, took one look and threw all our blankets and sheets on the floor.

"Now start again, you stupid load of shits!" he said, and snarled like a mad dog at us.

An hour later he let us go to the food tent to get some breakfast. We were hoping for hot rolls and olive oil. We got stale bread and margarine.

"Right, lads!" said the sergeant. "Get out to the square, on the double!"

We all shuffled outside, and it began to dawn on us that the stories about the army might have been true.

"Line up!" yelled the sergeant.

We all stood in a line standing as straight as we could. Shoulders back, head forward. The sergeant walked up and down, shaking his head. I must admit we did look a sight. Tall ones, short ones, fat and thin ones, all doing our best to stand to attention.

"Now, on my command I want you all to turn to the right… and RIGHT TURN!"

Some of us got a bit confused and some of us got the giggles. The sergeant was not happy. Not all of us could remember what was left and what was right. Was it our left or his left? For another hour he had us turning left and right, left and right. I made a fist with my left hand so I would remember which way to turn. Then we had to march.

"You can forget about food, boys, until you learn to march like soldiers, you useless bunch of idiots!" he shouted.

"By the time we finally got in step and were swinging our arms in time, the dinner bell had rung.

"DISMISS!" he bellowed. "You can go and eat now. Tomorrow is rope-climbing day."

Great, I thought, for that is something I am good at. We ran to the canteen tent. Big rolls with meat falling out of the ends were piled up on plates. I picked one up and took a big bite right in the middle. It was empty. I opened it up and at each end was a bit of meat. The rest was margarine. I looked up and caught the sergeant's eye.

"Welcome to the army, boys!"

"Lady Dee, your horses are in the lost garden," said Antonio.

"Oh bloody hell, the sods have gone walkabout," I replied in English.

We were walking the herds back from a long day on the hills in the *campo*, parallel to the river. I dashed to the edge and looked down. Yes, there they were, two English cobs heading back from the lost garden, walking along the river banks heading home.

Beau was, as usual, in the lead with Hardy following close on his friend's tail. I couldn't blame them for ducking under our electric tape and having a jolly upriver. It had been over three months since they had last ventured outside our land.

Felicity had popped over for a long weekend and we managed to grab an hour for a ride. We had to take care as the *campo* was full of olive pickers, dogs and children. We trotted along the track by the lost garden but, realising that the banging and shouting of the olive pickers would spook the boys, we turned around.

Fliss decided that a good fast canter in the lost garden would at least lift the spirits of horse, and rider. She and Beau took off, leaving me arguing with Hardy who wanted to engage in conversation with the olive pickers.

"Tally ho, young ladies!" he called. "Marvellous work, just the ticket."

"Hardy, move your fat arse," I said.

"Righto, old girl," he replied and broke into a high stepping cob trot.

"For goodness sake, Hardy, move! Beau is now out of sight."

He stopped showing off to the women, who by now had put down their 'boinking' sticks (sticks to knock the olives off the branches) to gaze at this great lummox of a horse.

Realising his friend (and compass) had disappeared, he bucked, farted, and took off. The sound of the fart must have ricocheted around the valley because, when we finally caught up with Fliss and Beau, both were in hysterics.

By the time the goats and I had reached the top of our track, leading to the farm, Beau and Hardy were crossing the river onto our land. The golden light heralding the coming of dusk had arrived, enveloping both boys. Chinni took the girls down the track while I stood, absorbed in this magical moment. The horses slowly moving into the light, triggered something in my brain.

Suddenly it seemed that the valley was filled with music, filled with Elgar, filled with *Nimrod*. It took my breath away and I let the tears fall.

14

The Canyon

There are two ways to enter the canyon and both are only possible in the height of summer when the river is low or dry. Approaching from Las Vicarias is the most difficult route. The river narrows with a sheer cliff on one side and a steep bank, leading into a dense wood, on the other.

We enter the canyon in the opposite and easier direction, following the river from Antonio's mill. The river narrows here. High, thick cane grass on both banks forms a tunnel which slowly widens. The light beyond guides us into the heart of the canyon.

Here the river chooses which way to flow. It can either cross the canyon floor, or dash off to fill up rock pools and meander around boulders before rejoining the main river.

I tiptoe across the pebbles to find a big rock to sit on and dry my feet in the sun. The girls climb up the far bank to eat and rest in the wood. Thankfully Alice has disappeared with the rest of the herd, leaving me to eat my last orange in peace. Chinni has already stationed herself in the wood so I can relax.

The huge cliff face in front of me is divided by a gorge. Many times I have watched mountain goats skip along the cliff, leaping effortlessly across the gorge and twirling in mid-air like ballet dancers. A year ago the scene was not so much Margo Fontaine and Rudolph Nureyev, more like a sequence from *Raiders of the Lost Ark.*

I should have known it was going to be one of those afternoons when I met up with Antonio by the river and saw the wide grin on his face. His goats were dashing around the eucalyptus trees, being chased by two new bucks.

"Who are they?" I asked

"Ah well, they jumped the fence from over the way," he said, waving in the direction of a big hill. "The old one is rubbish. But just look at the young boy."

A blonde buck raced past me in pursuit of Alice.

"Look at him, Diane. A pure Malaguenian boy." His grin was getting bigger. "New blood!"

"We can't keep them, Antonio. It's called theft."

"I'm not keeping that one," he said, pointing at the old smelly-rug with huge horns. "He is going back over the fence."

"How are we going to get him back over the fence?" I stared at the huge buck. "We can't catch him, let alone lift him."

I noted that he hadn't given me an answer regarding the question of theft.

"Don't worry. I have a plan."

"And what, Sir, is your plan?"

"You grab his beard and…"

"Bugger off! I'm not touching that!"

"Diane, when I grab him, you grab hold of his beard and twist."

"Okay, okay. But how are you going to catch him?"

"Ninja style," he said with a wink.

He crouched down and weaved his way through the herd, using the goats as cover. The big, hairy, smelly-rug was keeping out of the way of the other bucks. Antonio finally got close enough to grab the old boy's back leg.

"Quick! Grab his beard!"

The buck kicked and plunged forward. Taking a deep breath I

made a grab for his long, sticky tassel. Smelly-rug relaxed enough for Antonio to release his grip on the hind leg and then run around to join me.

"I'll hold his front leg and we can drag him to the fence."

"And then what?"

"We lift him over."

This was one very large buck, with horns, and the fence that we needed to lift him over was one-and-a-half metres high. I started singing the theme tune from *Mission impossible.*

"That's your plan?"

"Have faith, woman. Now hold his beard tight."

I twisted it another notch and Antonio let go of Smelly-rug's front leg. He dashed to his rucksack and pulled out his old denim jacket, placing it on top of the fence. He came back and again grabbed the buck's front leg.

"You hold him and I'll lift this front leg over."

I immediately saw a flaw in the plan.

"His horns will be at my eye level!"

"It'll be fine. Just move quickly."

He lifted one front leg over, resting it on the jacket.

"Left leg, Diane. Lift it now."

With one hand stretched out and holding tight onto his beard, I manoeuvered the other to move his left leg into position.

"Okay, let go of his beard and get behind him."

I let go. Antonio put his shoulder underneath the buck's chest and lifted him halfway over.

"Lift his back legs up and push him like a wheelbarrow."

I grabbed both back legs, lifted and pushed, Antonio coming to help. Two heaves and we had him tipped over the fence. The big, hairy, smelly-rug ran for the hills.

"What about the other one?" I asked, already knowing the answer.

"I'll never catch him. And anyway, he chose to be with my lot so it's not theft. So what shall we call him?"

I watched the new blonde bombshell dance around the goats, deftly avoiding Antonio's big boys.

"He is so handsome," I said. "There is only one name for him. Brad Pitt."

We spent the next three hours walking narrow goat paths on the hills, zig-zagging our way up the huge cliff that overlooked the canyon.

"Good herbs up here," said Antonio.

"We have to go down to the river soon," I said. "The goats are thirsty and I need to soak my hands in clean water."

I had gone through nearly a whole pack of wet-wipes to get the smell of the old buck's beard off my hands. I kept sniffing them and they still ponged of goat piss. I hoped that when I got home, a newly-acquired shower gel, care of a friend who recently stayed at a posh hotel, would do the trick. But for now, another scrub in the river may help to get rid of the stink.

"Soon, soon," said Antonio. "Let's have some fruit and rest a bit first."

I moved some rocks to clear a space to rest my weary body. Just as I was about to plonk my bottom on the flat ground, Antonio shoved me with his foot and I fell flat on my face.

"What the f..!"

"Scorpion," Antonio said, very calmly.

"Where is it?" I asked, jumping to my feet and hopping (for some ridiculous reason) from one foot to the other.

Antonio raised his stick and pummeled the ground.

"He has gone now. You can stop jumping."

"You killed it?"

"Yes, I killed it."

"You killed it?" I repeated.

Antonio never killed anything.

"It was your fault, Diane. You moved the stone so, in fact, it was you who killed it."

There was no answer to that. He was right. I finished a wedge of melon and felt guilty.

Time was moving on and we really needed to get down to the river.

"Antonio we must move. It will take us a good half hour to get down this hill."

"I have a plan Diane."

"Oh no! What is it this time?"

"We can climb down the gorge to the canyon," he smiled, daring me to argue.

I dared.

"We'll break our necks and those rocks at the top are not secure. It's far too dangerous."

"No, no, it will be fine. Those rocks haven't moved for years. We will be in the river bed in fifteen minutes." He gathered up his rucksack. "This is better than the long way, trust me."

I didn't trust him and I didn't trust the big boulders that were perched on the top of the gorge.

"The goats will dislodge them, Antonio. Use your brain."

"The mountain goats run over the gorge all the time. Come on, let's call the goats down."

The goats looked wary.

"They don't trust it, Antonio."

"Come on, we'll go first and your lot will follow."

He marched ahead. Gingerly I climbed down into the gorge, Antonio in the lead. He adjusted his straw cowboy hat and started the trek downwards. The slippery shale began to move. Antonio immediately took on a ski-slope stance, turning sideways with knees bent.

"Dig the sides of your feet into the shale," he called back to me, before whistling for the goats to follow.

They didn't. I looked up and saw the goats looking down.

"They won't come, Antonio. We have to climb back up."

He stopped skiing and looked up.

My blood turned cold when he muttered, "Oh, shit."

The goats had sensed danger and collectively started to leap across the gorge, all two hundred of them. The rumble started slowly as the first shower of rocks came down.

"Keep moving, Diane!" he shouted, as he upped his ski stance by jumping and digging his walking stick into the shale as rocks bounced past us.

"Move, Diane, move!" he shouted again. "Just keep jumping!"

I could barely keep upright. The rumble got louder and I knew what was coming. A huge boulder was chasing me, getting closer by the second. My brain froze but luckily my limbs took over. I ran and I jumped, trailing my walking stick for balance.

As soon as my feet touched the floor of the canyon, my legs pumped me away from the boulder and I ran through the river to safety. Before I turned around, I heard the crash behind me as the boulder smashed into a distant cousin and stopped for a chat.

Antonio rolled a cigarette and passed it to me. He hummed the theme tune from *Raiders of the Lost Ark*. I automatically took it. Two months off the tobacco, but at this moment I didn't care. I lit it and inhaled deeply. The dust settled.

"Where are the goats, Antonio?" I asked, scanning the cliff.

"Don't worry. Chinni and the Abuela will bring them back, they'll climb through the wood."

"It's too thick to get through. They'll get stuck,"

My voice was getting higher with every word.

"No, it's okay. The bucks will crash through."

He sat on a rock and tipped his cowboy hat to the back of his head.

"That was close," he said.

"Close? Close?" I spat out the words. """We could have been bloody killed!"

He rolled another cigarette.

"Diane, it was just another day at the office."

I thought about that, and yes, he was right. It was just another day at the office for a goatherder.

Feet dry, I slip my boots back on and climb the bank into the woods. Chinni has kept the herd together and they are now munching their way through bracken and vines. I find the big log that Antonio sometimes uses for a bed to sleep on when the heat of the afternoon becomes too intense, leaving me to take care of the herd. I sit down and open my rucksack to see if any food is lurking in the depths of my bag. Alice walks over to check.

"All the food has gone Alice," I lie, and she knows it.

"Okay, there may be a fruit bar left."

"Give it," she says, her eyes locking onto mine.

I manage one bite. Alice takes the rest.

August can be tricky. The heat is so intense you can hardly breathe. By 2 pm man and beast look for shade and attempt to sleep. Most of the goats are pregnant and produce little milk in this month. The search for good food can take up to nine hours a day.

Antonio would be nicely settled at the *molino*, trekking upriver, looking for fresh food to keep his expectant goats healthy and fat. I would have the whole valley to myself, away from Antonio's control and madcap ideas.

Occasionally we would meet up at the canyon if the temperature was too high to go further afield. It's a midway point between the *molino* and Las Vicarias. Antonio had phoned one hot Saturday morning, asking if I had his hoof trimmers.

"Yes, I have them," I said, feeling a little guilty.

I had promised to give them back to him after a hoof-trimming day the month before.

"I'll meet you at the canyon around 1 pm."

"Okay, I'll be there," I said into a dead phone.

Antonio gives orders. He forgets, or dismisses, the idea that I may have had other plans for the afternoon.

I set off at 11.30 am and kept close to the river bed. The girls were happy to go upriver for a change. I left the two sheep, Carmen and Loretta, at home. Also, I thought it best to leave a few special-needs girls behind as it was quite a long trek in this heat. I finally arrived in the canyon at the appointed time to find Antonio sitting on a log in the woods, eating his lunch.

"Want some?" He waved a slice of melon at me.

"No, I've got some sandwiches thanks."

I looked around to see if Alice was listening in. I pulled my trusty old sarong from my rucksack. Antonio never remarked how ridiculous I looked when I covered my head while eating. For me it's the only way to eat in this heat without adding fly to the menu.

"Have you finished? I need a ten minute kip and you are on my bed."

"Yep, all done," I answered. "I'll push off to the eucalyptus tree for a siesta. Ten minutes then?"

"Maybe twenty."

He lay down on the log, placing his straw cowboy hat over his face. He immediately began to snore.

I sat beneath a huge tree, knees to chin, turning my sarong into a tent. Then I also began to drift off. I don't know if I was asleep for five seconds or five minutes but something snapped my eyes open. I kept very still, ears straining for answers as to why I was so suddenly wide awake.

Was that thunder or an aircraft? I heard it again. Not wanting to awaken the goats or Antonio, I quickly and quietly unraveled myself from the sarong. I looked at the log but he wasn't there.

I found him by the river, sniffing the air and searching the clear sky. I stood next to him in silence. The rumble came again.

"Get the goats NOW, Diane!" he said, running to pick up his ruck sack.

I did the same.

"Run them through the river bed and then climb the bank to the road!"

I stood, blinking at him.

"Diane move! A flash-flood is coming! We have no time. I'll be behind you and make sure we have everyone."

I called my girls. Chinni sensed the danger.

"Girls, come on, run!"

We climbed into the semi-dry river bed. The quickest route out of the canyon was through the very narrow part of the river. This was dangerous but we had no other option. I began to run and I could hear Antonio shouting at the goats, urging them into the river bed. He sent his dog, Chivvi, into the undergrowth to check that he hadn't left any behind.

"Get up the bank now, Diane. NOW!"

I stopped running and directed Chinni to start climbing the steep bank up to the top track. She didn't hesitate. Both herds followed her. I started to climb the bank, Paz in front of me, showing me the best handholds. Behind me I saw Antonio running with one baby goat in his arms and another over his shoulder.

"Get up the bank, Diane, go, go, go!"

I got to the top and leaned down to take the youngster that Antonio had in his arms. The other was still perfectly balanced on his shoulders.

The goats, followed by the dogs, had run into an old olive grove, leaving Antonio, myself and the two baby goats who were having their first *campo* walk.

We stood and listened. All was quiet. I looked at Antonio and started to speak. He shushed me, his head cocked to one side, listening.

"Here it comes. Move back quickly!" he ordered.

I heard the cracking of cane grass, followed by a roar, as a wall of water raced past. It was terrifying. It thundered down the long cane tunnel, devoured the second bridge and continued around the sharp corner en route to Las Vicarias. I phoned Peter.

"Are the horses in the back paddock?"

"Yes, they were in already. I locked the paddock up when I heard the thunder. Are you okay?"

"Sort of. I'll tell you later."

We took the babies to the olive grove to find their mothers before returning to look at the river. I waited for Antonio's usual philosophical words, the grin, and the rolling of cigarettes. He skipped the first two and went straight for the smoke.

"Another day in the office, Antonio?"

"Both herds could have been wiped out, Diane."

This response surprised me. I tried another tack.

"We all survived. In a couple of hours the river will have gone down again and we can get the goats home." I smiled at him.

"I should have smelt that storm coming but I fell asleep."

This was new territory. Antonio always blamed me and any mistake he made, he covered with a joke.

"Never underestimate the river, Diane. Stay alert every day."

"I won't. I will stay alert."

"I'm serious Diane, very serious."

We went our separate ways, Antonio going over the big hills to the mill, while I took my girls over the opposite hill. By the time we both needed to cross the river, it would have subsided to a safe level.

This was my first up close and personal experience of a flash-flood. It was not to be my last.

15

Thumb

The herd is now sleeping in the dense wood above the canyon. I carefully climb the steep bank, trying not to disturb them. Chinni is resting her eyes under a huge eucalyptus tree and the 'family Alice' have commandeered four poplar trees for shade.

As little Eileen dares to rest her head on her mother, Willow is noisily chewing the cud, like a teenager with a mouthful of gum. Jennifer is laying out full-stretch, whilst her twin sister, Elizabeth, sits close, horns at the ready for anyone daring to disturb her sleeping sister. Her impressive horns once put me in hospital but also gave me a lovely day out.

We start milking around 6 am. Our small, solar-powered light just about held out for the first hour and by 8 am we were on our last batch of goats. Peter had tied up the 'family Alice' and, while he milked, I fetched two big mugs of coffee.

Entering the shed with the steaming brews in my hand, I smiled to myself, thinking that, just for once, we were ahead of schedule. Peter interrupted my thoughts.

"Oh shit! I need help, Diane!"

Elizabeth had tried to reach some grain beneath the feed trough. Her large horns were wedged beneath the trough and her collar, made from plaited bailing twine, was strangling her. She was unable to free herself.

I knelt down and held her horns. Pete produced his multi-tool from the depths of his combat trousers and tried to cut the twine free. Her eyes began to bulge. Peter cut as fast as he could, cursing a blade that was so blunt it couldn't cut through butter.

"Okay, she's free. Get her out, Diane."

I manoeuvred her horns, waggling them back and forth to free her. It was during those few seconds that the damage was done. Elizabeth took a deep breath and lifted her head, trapping my thumb against the sharp metal feed trough. She was free but I was in trouble.

"That bloody hurt, Elizabeth," I said in good humour.

I looked at my right thumb. I saw a trickle of blood and a gaping wound. Peter, totally unaware how serious the cut was, proceeded to call in the last ten goats to be milked. To prevent dust from entering the wound, I covered the hole in my thumb with my left hand.

"Peter," I said, my voice slightly higher than usual, "can you get some gauze from the first-aid box and then call Eileen?"

"Eileen?"

"Yes, our friend Eileen. Not the goat."

"Why? What's the matter?"

"I need to go to A&E rather quickly."

"No shit?"

"Yes, shit. Deep shit!"

I kept very still, not wanting the wound to bleed heavily. Then a thought struck me. I stank of goat.

"I've phoned Eileen. She'll be here in about twenty minutes. Can I see the damage?"

Pete knows that I hate hospitals so he figured it must be serious.

"No, no, you can't look. I need to sort myself out. You just carry on."

I walked slowly to the bathroom and with one hand managed to wipe off all the residual goat smell from my arms. I found a loose dress to wear and wriggled into it. A dash of lippy and a squirt of perfume (to at least try to keep up appearances) and I was ready for my dear friend to come to the rescue. I reached our gates just as her car skidded to a halt.

"What the hell have you done?"

"I've had a tiny accident, Eileen. I need to go to the Health Centre."

Eileen gave me a long hard look which I matched. She knew it was bad.

"Get in and don't bleed in the car."

Upon our arrival at the Health Centre, I kept the British stiff upper lip, smiling as I waved a blood-soaked, gauze-covered thumb. A nurse, ignoring my smiles, peeled off the dressing and examined the wound.

"Ronda hospital, now," she said.

"Ronda? Is that necessary?"

"Yes it is. You've severed your tendon."

"Bugger!" I said in English.

Eileen took the news in typical Eileen fashion.

"Shall we take the scenic route, Diane?"

"Yes please, nice and slow."

I don't get out much and so this little mishap enabled me to have a jolly. Eileen drove us through little hamlets where mules were being loaded up for a day's work in the *campo*. She slowed down when we passed a goatherder with his herd so I could smile and wave.

My thumb was throbbing a little but there was no pain. The views distracted me from worrying about what damage I may have done to my large digit.

We finally arrived at Ronda hospital and, within minutes, a doctor who resembled George Clooney ushered me into a cubicle.

He may have looked like a film star but sadly he left his manners in the dressing room. He focused rather on the fawning nurses.

"How bad is it?" I asked.

No reply.

"Coffee, doctor?" asked a slim, dark-haired young nurse.

"Thank you, Maria," he said with a smile, flashing perfect white teeth.

He swabbed my thumb then squirted brown and blue liquid around the wound. He gave me a couple of injections, to numb it, then disappeared stage right. Eileen, who was hovering outside, saw her chance to enter stage left.

"Where has he buggered off to?" she asked, staring intensely at my thumb.

"My best guess is that he's having a quickie with Nurse Maria."

"Your thumb looks a bloody mess."

"Thank you, friend, for those comforting words," I said.

The doctor came back.

"Outside," he ordered Eileen.

"Okay. Good luck, Diane. I hope he's washed his hands."

She left the room but remained outside the door, her nose pressed against the glass window. Nurse Maria handed Dr Love Machine a pack of stitches. Their eyes locked for a second.

Maybe it was my ego. Twenty years ago I might have been dazzled by that smile but now I'm just a middle-aged lady who stank of *Eau de goat* rather than *Eau de Chanel*. I had become invisible.

I stared at the doctor before staring at Eileen's face, squashed up against the glass.

"Twat!" I mouthed.

The only thing I could do to prove my worth was to watch intently as he sewed up my thumb. I may be a smelly old goatherder but I'm also hard.

Stitching finished, he thrust a sheet of paper in my hand and told me to make an appointment to have a cast fitted. That done, Eileen and I made a dash to her car and zoomed off to the nearest *venta* (café). We sat underneath a beautiful arch of bougainvillea, sipped coffee and shared a bowl of chips.

"Thanks, Eileen, this is a lovely day out."

"You're very welcome," she said. "Next time you need a hospital, we'll make a full day of it."

A year later she kept her promise.

Stitches out and cast put on, I was trying to work out how I could continue to help hand-milk the goats. Peter had to get up an hour earlier to get the milking finished in time to deliver it to the cheese factory.

"I'm going to try and milk Gerona," I said in a tone that he dare not argue with.

Our three-legged girl would surely understand my predicament. Hooking my cast around both her teats and, with a bucket clasped between my feet, I began to milk. Swoosh, swoosh came the steady flow and then my left hand cramped up. I rested for a few minutes and then tried again. I finally swooshed the last milk from her teats, pushing through the pain.

"There you are!" I said triumphantly. "I did it!"

Peter had milked five to my one.

"That's great, Diane, one less for me to do."

"I'll make coffee and then I'll have a go at milking Gina."

Putting the pan on the stove I noticed that my left hand was stuck in the shape of a claw. It was no use. My milking days were over, at least for a while.

Never mind, I thought, *I can still walk the goats*.

Antonio had rescued a small, black buck named Manolo. He had been kept in a tiny paddock for the first year of his life and was not used to *campo* life, let alone walking out into the great wilds of Andalucia. Antonio had sent him down to me.

"My boys will murder him. He is safer with you."

Manolo slowly began to accept the changes in his life. He made friends with my girls and kept out of the way if any arguments broke out in the herd. He did, however, have one odd quirk. He was afraid of heights.

Antonio didn't believe me until he took my herd out for a walk while I was in Ronda hospital having my cast fitted.

"Diane, he really is scared of heights. I had to push him over a tiny gorge today because he was too scared to jump."

"I told you!"

"It will pass," he said with great confidence. "He's a goat. It's natural to jump."

It didn't pass but we must embrace life's little oddities.

Peter needed a break from the goats to get on with other jobs around the farm. I needed to feel I was doing my bit, cast or no cast. I decided I would take my girls out with Antonio.

"What's the plan for today, Maestro?" I asked, waving my cast in the air.

Antonio took no notice of the cast. He had zero tolerance of people who moaned about their illnesses or problems. He had once had a very bad accident while fifteen feet high up a poplar tree. Chopping down a branch, he missed and sliced his knee with his axe. He climbed down the tree, wrapped his vest around the wound and continued.

His wife, horrified, had dashed him to the emergency department at the Health Centre to be stitched up. The only complaint he made to me was about the tetanus injection they gave him in his backside.

"Today we're going to go upriver. Because it'll be very hot, we'll keep to the river banks."

That was perfect for me. No hill work, just meandering for hours alongside the river. We started off at 11:30 am, slowly making our way past the *molino* before working our way to his father's olive grove that nestled close to the river bank.

"I'll go ahead along the bank to protect the olives, while you take them upriver," he instructed.

"Are you sure Antonio? That stretch of river can get very deep."

"Just climb over the rocks, Diane!"

He turned and walked away, forgetting I can't bloody climb. Had he forgotten my hand was in a plaster cast, and had he forgotten that I can get bloody angry? Apparently, he had as I was left alone with two hundred goats and a river to walk.

Thankfully I had my 'walking in the river' pumps on. I sloshed my way through the warm water while the goats kept, as best they could, to the river bank, jumping from rock to rock so as not to get their hooves wet. All the goats, that is, except Manolo. He happily trotted behind me until disaster struck.

I spotted a deep section in the river and carefully climbed over a great rock to avoid it. Manolo didn't see it and slipped into a deep pool which had an overhanging rock.

"Swim, Manolo!" I shouted. "I can't get you out!"

As he began to flounder I realised what had happened. Antonio had made an upside-down saddle for him. It's a rubber saddle to stop the bucks mating out of season. Manolo had got used to this odd contraption but now it was drowning him. One of his hind legs was caught in a saddle tie.

I climbed into the river, my trusty walking stick in hand. I needed to hook the tie and release his back leg. I got as close to him as I could without sinking into the deep sandy water. By now it had turned a muddy brown colour due to Manolo's thrashing. I prayed out loud and thrust the hooked end of my walking stick into the water.

Evidently my prayers were answered. I hooked the strap and Manolo pulled his back leg free. I then hooked his neck, which aided his climb out of the pool and onto a rock. He now had to climb like the other goats to avoid any other deep pools. Now it was my turn to scramble up and over the boulders.

My pumps had no grip, my right hand was in a cast and my left hand occasionally turned back into a claw. Apart from that it was a Mardi-Gras. When I finally arrived at the olive grove, soaked in blood, sweat and tears, the herd was already asleep in the shade.

"What kept you?" asked Antonio.

The few brain cells that were still functioning screamed at me to hit my friend over the head with my plaster cast. Pithy comebacks danced in front of my eyes. Words that would adequately vent my spleen began to form amid the dark recesses of an otherwise glittering intellect. Finally they paraphrased themselves into an apt retort.

"Antonio... Just eff off!"

It took a few weeks for Manolo to get over his near-drowning experience. I kept the goats close to home, weaving in and out of the cane grass by the river, trying to persuade Manolo that the river really was okay.

The herd desperately needed to eat some herbs high on the hills, but I didn't want to go onto Antonio's hills. Since the river incident I was barely speaking to him. The big hill behind our house would have to do.

Monty and Paz were not impressed when I called the goats to the foot of the hill. Mastin and water dog were enjoying a splash in the river, jumping on frogs and keeping cool.

"Mummy, is it entirely necessary to climb a bloody hill in this heat?" Monty asked, staring at me. His Prince Charles accent seemed to echo around the valley but only I could hear it.

"Don't look at me like that, Monty. Goats need herbs so up we go."

Paz then chimed in.

"Mum, you 'aven't been up there for ages and you're not very good on your feet."

I ignored her cockney voice. She is over protective. I was more than capable, even if my sense of direction was a tad off sometimes.

"Paz, guard those bottom olives and I'll lead them up."

I snaked my way along the goat paths which were overgrown with herbs. The goats were in heaven. I kept an eye on Manolo and he kept his eye on me. The rest of the herd had climbed high above me.

I tried to keep to the old pathway but as I rounded a corner I realised that Paz and Monty were no longer in front of me. I must have taken a wrong turn. To this day I don't know how this happened.

I probably drifted off into my usual fantasy world where I considered which goat would be best to ride if she turned into a horse. I realise that might sound rather odd but most goat owners who also ride horses will admit they do the same.

I was in trouble now because the path had narrowed. The left hand side was a sheer drop while the right was becoming more vertical by the second. I told myself that it would be okay as long as I didn't look down.

It was then that my feet began to slide from underneath me. I had no grip and, with my right hand in a plaster cast, I couldn't grab at any root or branch sticking out from the bank.

I had to think quickly. Maybe if I turned back along the path, on my hands and knees, I might find firmer ground. I chanced looking behind me and saw Manolo, his eyes wide with panic. He had followed my route along the narrow path.

I dropped into a crawling position, hoping my knees would keep me from sliding off the edge. Then I realised that this was not an option. Manolo would soon be on top of me and he would tip me over the edge. As I started crawling forward, the path began to narrow even more and my left foot slipped over the edge.

Paz and Monty must have been in deep conversation not to have noticed that I wasn't behind them. I imagined the following conversation between them:

"Nice breeze has come up now, eh Monty?"

"Well yes. One must savour these little pleasures in such a hostile environment."

"Have you seen Mum?"

"Look, Paz, the woman is probably hugging an olive tree or talking to some pesky lizard."

"Monts, I can't see her. Get your long nose in the air."

"Well, I have got a hint of something of her from below but it's mixed in with macho-boy smelly-buck."

"Oh, gawd! She's only gone and got herself bleedin' lost again!"

Paz would have checked the direction in which Monty's great

nose had pointed, looked down, and seen the catastrophe that was about to unfold.

"Go, Monty, go! She'll be a gonner in a few minutes!"

I clawed my fingertips into the dry earth, trying to get some sort of grip. It was impossible. I dug my chin into the path and closed my eyes, trying hard not to cry in frustration.

Suddenly, I felt something swish in front of my face. It was Monty's long, black tail. I grabbed it with my left hand and he started to pull. Using my cast as an ice axe I hauled the rest of my body along the path. Monty pulled, waited then pulled again. He had walked backwards along the path to get to me, realising it was too narrow for him to turn around.

He used all of his mighty strength to pull me to safety. The path widened and the ground became firm. Paz was waiting for us, cheering us on. As I reached Paz, Manolo leaped over my prone body, shaking with terror.

I lay still for a moment, still clutching bits of hair from Monty's tail. Paz went into nurse mode, cleaning my bleeding knees, before the three of us sat together.

I had no words to express my thanks to my two friends who had rescued me. I was physically and emotionally spent. I rested my head on Monty's shoulder, pulled Paz into my lap and wept.

16

Angels

The time has come to leave the canyon. Chinni leads the way down the long deep tunnel of cane grass to the second bridge. I bring up the rear, after checking all the goats have woken up and joined the herd. When I finally catch up with the girls, Chinni has them bunched together on the bridge.

"We're heading home, Chinni, nice and steady."

Chin is back on duty. She has to walk the herd past olive trees, a small vegetable garden and an orange grove. She heads off and I stay at the rear, checking that Willow hasn't crept off into the olive grove near the track. Alice's daughter has a habit of going her own way.

Far in the distance, Antonio's big hill looms. It was there that Paz, my little cockney-voiced water dog, showed me, yet again, what a professional she is.

The heat in July and August drains every fibre of one's being. The smallest of tasks saps one's energy and sleep patterns have to change. Milking starts at 5 am and it takes less time because most of the goats are pregnant and slowly drying up.

With Antonio now in the *molino*, his summer residence, I can take my girls all over the valley. By leaving at 10 am I can bring them home by 3 pm, which means that Pete and I can try and grab an hour's siesta.

One particularly hot, July morning I decided to take the goats to the canyon. There they would find good food, good shade and, with luck, I'd be home by half-past three.

Everything was going well. We stayed in the lost garden for over an hour before slowly making our way upriver to the second bridge. Monty kept close to me and Paz kept the girls from diving into the olive groves and orange orchard.

It was only when I arrived at the second bridge that I discovered a few were missing. Apparently Willow and half a dozen of her idiot followers had gone walkabout. I informed Paz who quickly retraced our steps downriver to find them. She returned empty-pawed.

I double-checked the herd again and found that, not only the idiots, but four very young girls were also missing. Paz rarely made a mistake and searched frantically for the goats.

Chinni moved the herd into the shade of the cane tunnel. Monty immersed himself in a pool of cool water. Paz and I were left to find Willow and the idiots and decide what to do next. We came to the same conclusion. Willow had veered off across the river, when we left the lost garden, and had headed for Antonio's big hill.

Paz stepped forward and scanned the great hill in front of us. I retrieved my small binoculars from my rucksack and yep, there she was, just a speck on the hillside with the others close behind her. Paz looked at me and I met her gaze.

"Sorry, Paz. I am so sorry."

"Don't you worry, Mum. I'll be off now."

My little girl ran to the hill, disappearing in a cloud of dust. She had crossed two olive groves before I had time to focus my binoculars on her. She, now a tiny black speck, climbed straight up the steep hill. I could just about make out Willow, Robyn, Daisy and Enya but not the youngsters.

The goats saw Paz coming and luckily bunched up together. They knew they were in big trouble. Paz was on top of them and pushed them down the hill at speed. I can only imagine the swear words my little cockney girl must have used to get them moving that fast. She was angry and the goats knew it.

I briefly lost sight of them, as they raced to the bottom of the hill, but then I tracked them by the dust cloud that they kicked up. Moments later the goats ran past me into the safety of the cane grass and the herd. Paz also flew past me and jumped into a puddle of water close to where Monty was sleeping. She drank and cooled her body.

I waited for a few minutes before I spoke.

"Paz, the youngsters are still up there."

Her big, brown eyes gazed into mine and she knew what she had to do. I was mortified to send her up again in this punishing heat but I had no other choice. I could turn the herd and push them up the hill. But it was over forty degrees and I couldn't ask pregnant girls to face that climb.

I considered phoning Antonio. Probably not a good idea because he would only get angry and tell me what a terrible goatherder I was. Paz stood up from her cool bath, shook herself and set off towards the hill. I watched her through the binoculars as she slowly climbed. She was obviously tired and suffering from heat exhaustion.

Higher and higher she climbed, passing the youngsters who were huddled under an old olive tree. Then the penny dropped. She wasn't tired, she was using her brain. Youngsters spook easily and instinct would make them split up and run higher. Until she was above their hiding place, she had to keep the four together and not frighten them.

She got into position and slowly made her way down to the kids. They began moving downwards with Paz shadowing their every move. It was painfully slow but my girl didn't make the mistake of rushing them. Finally they reached the bottom and disappeared from view. I could help by calling them.

"Come on, babies, we are over here. Come on!"

Paz pushed the pace up a notch and now all four were galloping towards me, screaming for their mothers. She dashed past me again and fell into the pool of water. With legs outstretched, she sprawled next to Monty, cooling down her little body.

My loyal friend saved the day again. My incompetence as a goatherder had put my dog at risk of heat stroke. My guilt made me phone Antonio to confess.

"That's her job, Diane. She knows what she's doing."

"But it was my fault."

"Yes, it was your fault. Do better next time. Give her a nice sausage tonight, she will appreciate that."

I did. She had two. After she had eaten all her dinner and her extra treat, I held her tight.

"Thank you, Paz."

She licked my face, before falling fast asleep.

When the rain came later that year, we danced. Dust turned to mud and the earth drank. Antonio had decided to take both herds far into the *campo*. There was no hint of heavy rain that afternoon so it would be safe to venture further afield.

"There are a lot of olive trees to protect, so keep Paz busy," Antonio instructed.

It was hunting season. Monty usually has to stay at home because he doesn't take kindly to the camouflaged men with a 'let's shoot anything with a pulse' mantra. But it was Monday and the wildlife could breathe easy. No hunting is permitted on Mondays. We climbed down a bank into a bowl of lush green grass. An hour later it began to rain.

"Are we okay?" I asked Antonio, looking up at the grey sky.

"Yes, we are fine. This rain won't bring the river up much, but we should move the goats up onto the path before the grass turns to mud."

It had been a pleasant hour. For once Antonio hadn't criticised my goatherding skills. Today was different. Today he had his 'women are nuts' hat on.

"Why do women clean the house every day?"

"Don't look at me. I have no glass in my windows so it's pointless."

He wasn't looking for an answer. This was Antonio's afternoon rant.

"Every day's the same. They stand outside with a bucket of water to clean the *rejas* (bars) and the front door. Then, a tractor comes past and covers it all in dust again."

He finished rolling a cigarette, took a deep puff, and continued.

"It's all for show, nothing more."

"Is it not a habit copied from their mothers?" I ventured.

"Maybe, but it's now a competition to shame anyone who hasn't gone out in all weathers to clean."

"Shaming does sound a bit harsh, Antonio."

"Oh yes, shaming. Some women were talking outside my garage the other day and they were criticising a neighbour who hadn't cleaned her door for two days. I said to them that, maybe, she was unwell."

"What did they say?"

"*Nada* (nothing). Not a word. They just looked at me as if I was a flea and carried on talking as if I didn't exist."

I wanted to point out that the *campo* men do that to me all the time but he was now walking away, shouting instructions over his shoulder.

"You leave last. Keep the goats all together and protect the olives up at the top. I'll lead them down the track."

He whistled his dogs into action and 160 goats galloped up the bank. Paz was still sheltering under my rain coat. She poked her head out as Monty and I watched the stampede to the top track.

"Moving them too fast, Monts," said Paz.

"I think they're going too fast up the bank, Paz," I said to my little cockney dog.

"I've just said that, Mum."

Monty sat quite still, his regal head held high.

"Paz, she can't hear you. You're speaking out of her range, darling."

My two friends were staring up at the fast-disappearing herd. I needed to get moving myself.

"Paz, let's go and protect those olives or we'll be in trouble with Antonio. Off you go and I'll catch up."

Paz gave me a quick glance and scampered up the bank, Monty hot on her heels. I checked that all goats had left the 'salad bar' and I began to climb the bank to catch them up. I slid down. The goats had turned the bank into mud. Moving along to find a less treacherous route, I tried again. Two steps up, and back down I came. I began to get the giggles.

"This is ridiculous," I told myself. "Just climb the sodding bank!"

I kicked my Wellington boots into the earth and dug my fingers into the mud, hauling myself up. Nearing the top, I came face to face with Paz. Our eyes met as I slid back down to the bottom.

"I can't get up, Paz." My laughter was now sounding a tad hysterical.

"I can see that, Mum."

"I'll keep trying Paz, you guard the olives."

Paz disappeared from view and I dug my boots in again. I clawed my way up the bank, pressing my knees, elbows and chin into the earth, hoping that at least one part of my anatomy would get some sort of grip. I looked up. Paz and Monty were looking down.

With my body now clinging to the bank, but slowly sliding down, Monty came to the rescue. Front legs over the bank, he lowered his head. I took a deep breath and made a grab for his collar. He pulled back and I dug one boot a notch higher in the bank. He pulled again and my left hand reached the top. One more pull and I crawled over the top.

"Thank you, my dear friends. I honestly don't know what I would do without you."

"You're welcome, Mum!"

Paz and Monty turned and quickly walked along the track to find Antonio. I tried to keep up but was hampered by two inches of thick mud clinging to my Wellington boots. 'Little and Large' were in deep conversation.

"It's time she retired, Monts."

"You're quite right. She could take up knitting or something, the poor dear."

"She could but I bet she'd be crap at that too."

Both dogs stopped, waiting for me to catch up.

"Lesson number 642 of goatherding is to get up the bank before the herd," I said to my lovely, furry chums.

Paz and Monty looked at me, obviously pleased that I was still laughing and in a positive mood, even though I was covered from head to toe in mud. Bless them.

"She could try painting by numbers, Monty. She couldn't possibly go wrong with painting by numbers."

To cuss, blaspheme, use expletives or 'swear like a trooper' are all allowed deep in the *campo*. The 'F' word, when I lived in England, would be muttered under my breath with only the 'you' in audible range. My friend, Matt, gave me a little booklet, at our leaving bash in England. It was titled, *Essential Foreign Insults*.

One cold and rainy winter evening, Peter and I studied this little gem over a bottle of wine. We concluded that profanities were best voiced in Esperanto, as nobody in the world would have the faintest idea what we were on about.

For example, 'tosser' in French, is *branleur*. In German it is *wichser*, and in Spanish, *gilipollas*. But in Esperanto, it is *fingrumo*.

Perhaps it's just us?

I memorised 'Your mother was a hamster, and your father smelt of elderberries' in Spanish but, as yet, have not used it.

Antonio insisted that we walked the goats close to the main road. My nerves were in a million pieces by the time we finally veered away from the crash barrier along the side of the road.

"I'm not ever doing that again, Antonio," I said, stealing his roll-up just as he was about to light it. This was the umpteenth time this year that I had failed to quit.

"Calm yourself, Diane. No one got killed," he said, calmly rolling another cigarette for himself. "Just one more little road to cross and we'll be back in the *campo*."

With no traffic visible, Antonio led both herds across the small road and onto a track, leading to good new grazing. I stood in the middle of the road, just in case a car happened by, and Chinni stood with me. As the last of the goats were crossing, a four-wheel drive came tearing towards us.

I stepped forward and motioned him to slow down and wait. As the truck slowed and I smiled to thank him, he crunched his gears and drove at Chinni. She wasn't moving but I did. Leaping in front of the bull bars I banged my hand on the bonnet and yet he still moved forward. It was then that a torrent of swear words left my mouth. A character from a Quentin Tarantino movie would have been impressed. Although delivered in a Kentish accent, the driver appeared to get the gist.

Antonio ran back from the track to see what on earth was happening. Thankfully he arrived just I was going into full 'Basil Fawlty mode', banging my walking stick against the driver's door. Grabbing it from me, he waved the driver on.

"Are you crazy? You can't beat up a car!"

"That *fingrumo* was going to drive into Chinni!" I yelled, by now quite close to tears.

"Oh. That's okay then," he said, patting me on the back.

That was the last time I took my girls close to the road.

It had rained, on and off, for a week. The river was up but we could still cross the little bridge to find grazing on the hills. Antonio had taken his herd close to the road. Pete came to the bridge with me to make sure that everyone crossed safely. We arranged that on my phone call he would meet me on my return to help the goats safely across again.

The hills were greening up and the paths were not too muddy. In the distance I spotted a wooded area. Why hadn't Antonio taken the goats there before? From a distance it looked a wonderful eating place, with lots of bracken and herbs. Monty, Paz and I picked up speed to overtake the herd and look for a pathway down to this new restaurant.

We found an overgrown path and I called for the girls to follow me. It was a steep path and the bracken was very thick, so I called the girls again to follow me. As I turned my head to see what was keeping them from charging down the path, my feet began to slide.

I tried to regain my balance by clutching at bracken and digging my walking stick into the earth. I was aware that I was on the 'down' escalator towards the edge of a cliff. I sat, using my bottom to slow me down. I dug my heels into the path that had now turned into shale but the escalator kept moving.

The only chance I had of surviving this ride was to aim for a big rock just by the edge of the cliff. I rolled over twice, to line myself up. As my feet hit the target I took a deep breath, and spat out the only word my dry mouth could muster.

"Bollocks!"

So much for swearing in Esperanto!

Paz had stayed on the top path with the goats and Monty was now working his way down the path to rescue me. My dog would be at risk trying to save me all because of my own stupidity. I had to climb higher. I flipped over on to my front, and crawled on all fours to reach the higher path.

"Wait there, Monty," I called out, as the big dog was about to leave the path and come to me. "Let me get away from the edge."

I had to crawl sideways to get to the path and it was slow going but Monty was ready. He lowered his head and I made my move. My knees were screaming in pain and again I began to slide down towards the cliff edge. I shot my right hand out and found his big, red collar. He pulled back, taking my full weight. I dug my toes and knees into the earth to help him.

He finally hauled my battered old body up onto the path and solid ground. Monty lay down in front of me, and we were nose to nose. For a moment he comforted me and I thanked him. I expected to see Paz and a herd of mocking faces but they were nowhere to be seen. They must have run back to the bridge.

Terror clouded the pain in my knees and hands as I played out a scene in my head of a young goat falling off the bridge and drowning. Or maybe of Carmen being tipped off the bridge and the weight of her wool dragging her down. I quickly climbed up to the top path and started to run, Monty hot on my heels. The phone rang. It was Eileen.

"Hi, I'm just checking in. Have you eaten and taken the vitamin tablets I gave you?"

"Oh, hello Eileen," I said trying to sound jolly. "All is fine, well, sort of. Nearly killed myself again and now I'm running after the goats."

"I'll call again in ten minutes."

My knees were begging for mercy as I ran up and down narrow goat paths but still there was no sign of the herd. My imagination was now in overdrive.

I finally reached the small olive grove close to the river and there they were. Paz had held them together, waiting for me and Monty to arrive. She had had no doubt that her friend would rescue me.

I believe that the universe sends angels down to protect us as we stumble through this life. Whoever is in charge of allocating these angels must have thought it best to err on the safe side, and sent me two. The phone rang, it was Eileen. I smiled.

Make that three.

17

Lilith

Early evening and the bee-eaters are now out in force, swooping around the herd collecting insects like a squadron of spitfires. I stand, as usual, mesmerised by their aerial display and then Alice breaks rank.

"Alice, move away from the orange tree now!" I shout, lobbing a handy stone at her.

The 'family Alice' reluctantly follow the rest of the herd. Chinni is now leading the girls up the cliff path towards the lost garden while I run like a demented scarecrow along the orange grove boundary. I know Chinni will hold them at the lost garden. She will wait until I catch up to give instructions.

Like Paz, who lets me believe that I'm in charge, Chinni quietly sorts out my mistakes. She stands by my side, in solidarity with the idiot woman who likes to call herself a 'lady goatherder'.

I am sure Peter thinks that I exaggerate Chinni's abilities, my love for her embellishing her talents. However, he finds out that everything I tell him about Chinni is true. He finds out when Lilith appears in our life on the farm.

At first I thought it was wind, or perhaps a reaction to my new *M&M* sweet craze. A sudden pain would spring up on my right side, severe enough to have me clutch at it, double over and swear very loudly. The pain came in spurts for about a year and then it became constant.

"Could it be your appendix?" Peter suggested.

"Of course not," I snapped. "People my age do not get appendicitis."

"Time for the doctor, Diane," he said. "You can't keep on self-diagnosing."

I relented. We would go after milking in the morning. I started to feel ill during the night, really ill. I had a tummy upset and was sleeping in the room close to the loo. I woke around midnight, in a pool of sweat, and then began shaking.

I had no strength to walk across the yard to wake Pete, only enough to pull the big duvet around me. I was scared and couldn't work out what was happening. I drifted in and out of sleep until 8 am when Pete came in to wake me.

"I've nearly finished the milking. Are you okay?"

"Yes, fine. Well, no actually, I need the A and E."

Pete finished milking the goats as fast as he could. He phoned our friend Anne Marie to meet us at the Health Centre. We needed a fluent Spanish speaker to make sure we didn't miss anything in the diagnosis.

I lay down on the examination bed with Anne Marie holding my hand. She knew I was in trouble as my British upper lip had started to droop. The doctor prodded me and I went through the roof with pain.

"Ronda immediately. It's her appendix," the doctor told Anne Marie.

Pete guided me back to the car and Anne Marie tucked me into the passenger seat.

"Back to the farm, Pete," I said.

"Are you bloody mad, we're going straight to Ronda Hospital!"

"The farm Peter, I need stuff to take."

I decided not to explain to my husband that I needed a leg shave and hair wash. He wouldn't understand. Peter phoned Antonio to come down and collect the goats for their afternoon walk while I locked myself in the bathroom.

The pain was getting more and more intense. With my legs badly shaved, hair cleaned, radio and books packed, I was ready to make the forty-five minute journey to the hospital.

"Are we nearly there yet?" I asked Pete.

"Not long now," he said, gently increasing the car's speed.

We arrived and I didn't have to wait long before a doctor ushered us into a room. He prodded my right side. My hand flew out and grabbed his wrist.

"No, no. Don't touch," I said.

"Okay, I will now just touch your left side," he said.

He pressed and again I grabbed his wrist. That hurt too. Much more than it should have done.

He made a phone call and a nurse appeared with a wheelchair.

"You need a scan in a big machine," he said, slowly and loudly.

I gave Pete a wave as the nurse wheeled me at breakneck-speed along corridors to the body-scanner room. Half an hour later I was back with the doctor.

"Your bowel has wrapped itself around the appendix," he said, trying to explain using hand gestures.

Had I not been in so much pain I would've been in hysterics just watching him. I suppressed it with a snort that he mistook for a pain-ridden groan.

"Are you going to operate today?" Pete asked.

"Oh no. *Dios*, it is too dangerous. Your wife needs antibiotics and other drugs for ten days first."

"So, do we collect the drugs from the Pharmacy?" I asked.

He stared at me and I stared back with a beaming smile that hopefully hid the pain. Now realising that I was quite mad, he turned again to Peter.

"She will be here in hospital for ten days. A bed is being made ready now."

As if by magic, the nurse appeared and I was wheeled again at high-speed along corridors with Pete running to keep up. We arrived at a room which had only one other bed occupied. Drips were being arranged to stick into me and I thought it best that Pete now buggered off back to the farm to sort out Antonio and the animals.

"Pete," I called after him. "Tell Antonio that I've named my appendix."

"You've named it?"

"Yep. Its name is Lilith."

Eileen had been to England for a week, visiting her granddaughter. I didn't think it was necessary to inform her that I was in hospital because she would have caught an early flight back. She always phones me when she gets back to Spain.

At Malaga airport, she will dash through arrivals, light up a cigarette and phone Frank, her husband, who is waiting in the car park. She will then phone me. On this occasion, she phoned me a few days after I was hospitalised.

"I'm back," she said drawing heavily on her cigarette.

"Great, I'm in bed," I said, trying to sound jolly.

"What the hell are you doing in bed? Are you ill?"

"Yes, a little bit ill. Well, a lot actually. I'm in Ronda Hospital."

She must have just inhaled a second time as all I could hear was coughing.

"What have you broken now, you bloody idiot?"

"You remember my wind problem? Well, it turns out it was my appendix, aka Lilith."

"Okay, what do you need?"

Eileen had immediately kicked into looking after her twit of a friend.

"Some soup for Pete, or an evening meal. Don't worry about me as I have room service."

"Diane, I have one word for you, my friend."

I braced myself.

"TWAT!"

"I know, I know. But the upside of all this is that I get three meals a day and no washing up."

I knew she was smiling as she rang off.

With Eileen on cooking duty, my concern now was whether Peter could handle the herd. He had Paz and he had Chinni. Would they help him as much as they had me?

"Is all well?" I asked, phoning mid-afternoon from the hospital bed.

"Oh yes, all is well," he answered, noisily munching on a sandwich.

"So, all the goats are grazing around you?"

"Yes, no, shit!

He must have swallowed a whole sardine and sounded like he was convulsing.

"Peter," I said, trying to sound calm, "where are the bloody goats?"

"I've got some of them… well, I've got four."

"Go and find them," I ordered. "I'll phone back in thirty minutes,"

I cut the call and fretted. They could have gone for miles. They could have climbed through the small gap in the fence that borders a huge estate. They could have dashed to the good olive grove on the other side of the hill. A bloody wolf might have appeared and devoured them. Aliens may have abducted them. I was going crazy with worry. The phone rang.

"I've got them. You were right about Chinni. She came back to find me just as you rang off. She stood in front of me and shook her horns before turning around and going back up the hill. I followed her with the old girls following me. The rest of them were grazing just around the corner."

Chinni had not let me down. She knew that the other human was also an idiot and that, for the next ten days, while I was in hospital, she would take charge.

Peter fed and milked the girls, swept out stables and put down clean chippings. The rest of the day he took his instructions from a goat.

Lilith was now subdued and the doctor told me that I could be discharged.

"Sorry, did you say discharged?" I asked, repeating the words very slowly.

"Yes, you go home tomorrow."

"But Lilith, I mean my appendix. Is it being removed?"

"Yes of course, but not yet," he said, backing out of the door. "The nurse will give you papers and instructions before you leave in the morning." He turned and bolted before I could ask any more questions.

The day after I arrived home, Peter drove me to our friends' bar. I had arranged to meet Eileen and Anne Marie to read and translate the paperwork I had been given. Pete and I couldn't make head nor tail of it.

I ordered toast and coffee and out came a huge bacon roll. Ian and Laurie, the bar owners, have always taken care of us. When they knew money was tight, an extra sausage would be put on our plate. He would inform us that Laurie had cooked one too many and that it was a shame to let food go to waste. Ian is a terrible liar but a very kind friend.

"So what's the instruction?"

"Well, in a nut shell, Diane," said Anne Marie, trying to suppress her laughter, "you have to have a camera up the botty."

Eileen spluttered out her coffee, not attempting to suppress her laughter. There was a split in the audience sitting at other tables. One lot sniggered and the rest nodded gravely in sympathy.

Eileen picked me up at 8.30 am on the dreaded 'up the botty' morning. Pete was still milking and had a long day ahead of him. We made good time and arrived at the hospital with five minutes to spare.

The procedure was interesting. I was drugged up sufficiently not to feel the camera, but could still shout a running commentary to Eileen who was pacing outside the door. I craned my neck to see the screen while the camera took a good look at Lilith. It wasn't a pretty sight.

A nurse, who seemed to me to be rather hostile, finally released me into Eileen's care. She practically shoved me out of the door. Luckily Eileen was ready to catch me as I swayed, still in shock, at the sight of Lilith on the big screen.

"Come on, I've prepared a picnic. Let's go and relax," said my friend as she gently guided me to her car.

True to her promise a year ago, after 'Thumb', she gave me a wonderful day out, with great views, food and coffee. We never mentioned Lilith once.

Food in the *campo* was getting scarce. Luckily for us and the goats it was olive pruning time. We had permission to collect all the cuttings from our neighbour's huge estate. Pete picked up a van load of the fresh cuttings and the girls were happy and full.

Chinni and Pete needed a rest from the sweltering heat and from walking for hours on end to find food. All now could enjoy a siesta.

My appointment finally arrived for the operation. All went well but people seemed to have lost their sense of humour. I merely asked the surgeon, before they were about to put me under, if it was possible to put the appendix in a jar for me to take home.

"*Senora*, the appendix has to be analysed."

For what? I thought. It's dead. No therapy or counselling would help. I could see that I needed to find a compromise.

"Is it possible for me to have half the appendix?"

"No!"

The gas mask came closer.

"Wait, wait," I implored.

"What?" demanded the short-tempered anaesthetist.

"Her name is Lilith."

He clamped the mask over my face and the lights went out.

Back at home, after spending a few more days in the hospital to recover, the animals seemed pleased to see me. Pete, on the other hand, was more cautious. I could see him bracing himself for the interrogation. He had sorted all the goats, the horses hadn't escaped and the dogs had been bathed and groomed. But I still couldn't resist.

"Did you remember to change the cat's water every day?"

"Yes."

"Cat litter?"

"Yes."

Just as I was about to ask another stupid question, he turned to face me.

"Everyone is alive, Diane, everyone survived. Now shut up and have a glass of wine, a beer or whatever will calm you down!"

I shut up and quietly filled the cat bowl with food. Eileen came for a fleeting visit, bringing cold beer, while Peter happily cleared off to collect more cuttings. We sipped the beer and I mused as Eileen walked up and down. She can never sit still. Pacing seems to give her the patience to deal with me.

"I mean, Lilith was with me for over 55 years, Eileen, so it is a bit of a loss."

"It nearly bloody killed you so good riddance to it, I say."

"True, true. But she was still part of me. When you think about it, my knees and back have played up for years. My teeth have caused me agony since I was a child. My bladder is very iffy since Felicity's birth. But Lilith has only been a problem for a year."

Eileen handed me another can of beer. She thinks I am truly bonkers but she accepts me. She gave me a long hard look before raising her can to clink with mine.

"To Lilith!" she said.

"To Lilith!"

18

Julio

Chinni waits at the far end of the long field that is known as the lost garden. The tall weeds and dry grasses are a perfect change of diet after hours of eating cane grass and bramble. I weave my way through the herd to join her.

"Go on, Chinni, go and eat, I've got this."

Checking that Alice is eating at the far end of the field, I quietly lower my rucksack off my aching shoulders and hide it behind a boulder. Although all the food has gone, it still holds emergency first-aid equipment, bandages, cotton wool, a plastic container full of wood-ash, Germoline, tweezers and rubber water-pipe. Carrying this weight came about because of a Mexican comedy actor, likened to Charlie Chaplin, named, 'Cantiflas'.

Antonio claims that when he names a kid, the correct name comes to him as soon as he touches the baby. That is not strictly true. He has fads. One year, the machos were named after boxers and martial artists but mostly he let the universe decide.

One young buck he named Tulipan, which in English is tulip.

Although sweet when he was born, Tulipan grew up to be rather miserable and quite ugly. Perhaps the universe thought he needed an edge in life. Then along came the pretty, tri-coloured, big boy. He spent his first few months leaping on and off Antonio's back during milking time.

"I have named him Cantiflas."

"Who is Cantiflas?"

"A very funny actor like Charlie Chaplin."

He grabbed his walking stick and did a very good impression of Charlie Chaplin's walk.

Cantiflas grew into a big, hefty buck, beautiful, gentle, and with the bonus of not having any horns. Julio, the brat, was now 'King' of the bucks. His horns, now fully developed and huge, had become a real problem. He was the only boy left who had these weapons.

Antonio had decided to only keep hornless bucks after Julio's earlier antics with us. Julio was quite aware that he had full advantage over the herd. The other bucks used their weight while Muhammad Ali employed his dancing skills to win a battle. But Julio fought dirty.

We had walked the goats over the hills on a lovely, breezy June afternoon. Julio picked a fight with Cantiflas. I took in the view as Antonio watched the bout.

"Shit, shit," he muttered, running towards the fighting boys.

I snapped back into action and ran after him.

"F— off, Julio!" he shouted, kung-fuing him right between the eyes.

"What's happened?"

"Broken front leg. I need a splint fast," he said, holding Cantiflas's leg out straight.

His eyes searched around and rested on my homemade cane walking stick.

"Hold his leg straight while I sort out a splint."

"What do I do if he tries to move?"

"Just hold the leg and gently pull down. It's a good clean break, it will be okay."

He grabbed my cane stick and, with his ever-sharp knife, went to work. He cut and trimmed two perfectly sized splints.

"Give me one of your socks," he ordered.

I worked out what he was going to do. Why it had to be my new white sock, that my mother-in-law had just posted over from England, I'll never know.

He cut the sock and between the two of us we threaded the sock over the broken leg. He placed the splints and I bandaged it with my ever-handy horse-wrap and poked cotton wool into the top and bottom for extra comfort. Cantiflas hadn't moved an inch. I was amazed.

"With a break, Diane, you have to move very fast," he said, rolling a ritual cigarette. "The goat is in shock and the pain hasn't kicked in yet."

Cantiflas tested the ground with his bandaged leg and felt confident enough to hop back to the herd.

"Give me Monty's collar and lead. Julio is grounded."

We made our way back down the hill and headed for home. Cantiflas quickly adjusted to his splint and negotiated the downward climb with ease.

"Six weeks and he should be mended."

Julio didn't object to having a collar and lead. In fact he calmed down and was enjoying the attention Antonio was giving him.

"There is something wrong with him," Antonio said quietly.

"He looks fine to me. I mean, he has just broken Cantiflas's bloody leg in a fight."

"I don't know what it is. He has no symptoms of illness but there is something not right. I just know it."

A few months later his fears were confirmed.

Replenishing my first-aid kit with rolls of cotton wool and vet-wrap, Peter presented me with four halves of strong plastic water pipe to add to it.

"There you go, two sizes, smooth edges. Will work much

better than cane for a broken leg," he said, rather proudly. "I'm amazed that the genius that is Antonio hadn't thought of this before."

Working alongside my neighbour sometimes left me feeling useless, stupid and totally inept.

One morning he had popped down to borrow my newly purchased bottle of anti-inflammatory medicine. We took it in turns to buy medicines, and share them, as they go out of date quite quickly.

I had been a little concerned about Patty, my best milker. She was never ill. Seeing her quiet and off her food at milking time worried me. I could find nothing wrong.

"Please have a quick look at Pat, She's not quite right and I can't figure out what the matter is."

Antonio walked into the paddock, looked at Patty for all of five seconds and said, "Get your tweezers, Diane."

By the time I returned, after diving into my trusty rucksack to find the tweezers, which were buried at the bottom of the bag, he had Patty in a gentle arm lock.

"There's a grass seed in her eye, Diane."

He removed a long seed from under her top eyelid.

"Put some antibiotic cream under her lid and she will be fine."

He walked away leaving me, yet again, feeling a complete failure. I had only just recovered from my March humiliation when I had three goats that were off-colour. I'd phoned Antonio.

"They have a tick somewhere on them," he suggested.

"I've searched for ticks. It's not ticks."

"Yes it is, look again hair by hair. A tick is on them, you just haven't looked properly."

An hour later, with my back screaming for mercy, I found tiny ticks on all three goats. Occasionally he threw me a grain of kindness.

"Diane, it's taken me thirty years to learn all this. You have to learn 'goat' and you haven't got that amount of time. You are doing well, don't worry."

He patted me on the back and I glowed with the praise.

"A good tip for you is that in tick season, you look for ticks and when grass seeds are on the floor, you look for grass seeds."

He giveth, and he taketh away.

"I don't know how he bloody does it," said Peter, after returning from helping Antonio move equipment around in the sheds. "Me, I need a certain size piece of wood to fix something and half an hour is lost looking for it. But him, he just glances around and whatever he needs appears, as if by sodding magic."

Pete was not exaggerating. I have watched him building things or mending something and when he needs a piece of wood or a handy half-metre-sized metal rod, it just appears right next to him. Okay, not by magic but hidden next to him on the floor.

So one rainy afternoon, when we were huddled in his sheds, waiting for a gap in the rain to walk the goats, I asked him.

"How do you manage to find everything you need. Is it pure luck?"

He pulled up a beer crate, sat, rolled a cigarette and explained.

"Everything you do in life you must do with intention. When I need something to help me I expect it to appear, and it does."

"So, is it a God thing?" I asked.

"A God thing?" he replied, shaking his head.

Antonio is not religious.

"It's inside you. With intention everything comes to you when you ask. You think it, and it happens."

The following week, Sandrine, a friend, gave me a book. It was titled *The Law of Attraction*.

Peter rarely gets any praise from Antonio. Maybe a nod of the head but that's about it. That was until the water tower arrived. It was a small but memorable moment that kept a smile on Peter's face for weeks.

Our water supply comes from a well located on the other side of our big field. Up until now it had pumped water into a concrete tank in the middle of the field. From there we had to collect it in water bottles, then use a wheelbarrow to ferry them to the house.

We needed a huge tower with a platform on the top to support a fibreglass tank. We could pump the water directly to the top of the tower and then pipe the water to the house and loo. We took a deep breath and ordered a five metre steel tower from the local metal works.

Three weeks later it was ready for collection and Antonio and Peter picked it up with the tractor and trailer. Rafael, who was lurking at Antonio's house, flagged down the tractor and hopped in. He was ready for an adventure and some free beer.

Peter had already prepared two deep trenches for the legs to drop into. The tower lay horizontally on the trailer and Antonio backed it up as close as he could to the trenches. He raised one end of trailer to slide the tower off.

Lowering the trailer to its horizontal position should have lifted the other end of the tower but it wasn't working. The trailer didn't have enough lift to push the thing upright. The two Spaniards shouted at each other, pushed, pulled and jumped up and down. Peter stood back and thought.

"The Englishman is thinking," said Rafael.

"What?"

"Look, look. Pedro is thinking."

Both stopped and stared at the Englishman.

"You need to rope it differently and drop the trailer down. That will bring the tower up," said the thinking Englishman.

Antonio rolled a cigarette as Peter re-arranged the ropes. He then nodded his head, eyes following the newly-tied rope.

"There you go, Antonio. Drop the trailer down, then nudge the tower while we pull the ropes."

A few moments later the tower fell into place. Rafael banged Peter on the back, surprised that an Englishman had out-thought a Spaniard. Antonio just smiled.

Our friend, Andy, helped Peter cement the tower legs in place and between them hauled the huge fibreglass tank up onto the platform. Andy ran pipes to the house and loo and arranged stand pipes for the animals' water. Andy is an expert. He and Julie live upriver and transformed a derelict house into a beautiful home.

They knew we were short of pennies and had few basic luxuries. He organised the labour and designed and built our kitchen, loo and shower room. While I was walking the goats, Julie tiled and painted. Their skills changed our lives. Our gratitude goes out to them for having made it all happen.

The water was turned on. We all stood together and turned on the kitchen tap, swiftly followed by the first flushing of the loo. We all did a happy dance before opening the wine.

Julie and Andy had been there. They had had to make do with a 'bucket' shower, over a pallet, whilst living in a small caravan. They knew what this meant to us.

I go into town with Pete three or four times a week. He drops off the milk at the cheese factory and I drink coffee at a bar, use wi-fi, and meet up with friends. It is a welcome break.

Working with Antonio everyday can be draining. I rack every brain cell trying to keep up with his machine-gun Spanish. The hourly chat with English friends in the bar is so relaxing. Anne Marie and Zoe, the local estate agents, often bring new clients to the bar to question us old timers.

New house-owners can be fun. You meet them on their first trip over, all fresh and bouncy. By day five, the frustration of shops shutting down for the afternoon, just as a packet of grout is needed, gets to them. By day fourteen, calmness and smiles return. It's Spain and they learn to go with the flow and have an afternoon kip.

Many of the 'newbies' ask where they can buy a little dog and all the stories are similar. Before permanently moving to Spain, they'd waited until their old dog had gone up to doggie heaven. But life without a dog just didn't feel right.

"How do we go about getting a dog?" they ask, their eyes following every pooch passing by.

"Oh don't worry," we tell them, "one will turn up in a few days."

Sure enough, a couple of weeks later the 'newbies' walk proudly into the terrace bar with a little dog on a lead.

"You were right. Minnie just sat outside our door, thin and full of fleas. We asked the neighbours if anyone owned her and they just shrugged their shoulders."

Minnie, by now, is ensconced on a 'newbie' lap, clean, groomed and sporting a pink collar and lead. We smile and pat little Minnie.

"We've had her micro-chipped and jabbed, she's ours now!" says Minnie's beaming mum.

After they leave, the bets are on.

"Two months," I say.

"No, no," chimes in Austin, "it will be at least three months after the hunting season."

"One week. I've spotted a new one in town," says Anne.

Nine days later, 'Newbie' walks to the bar with little Minnie and large Rinty.

He is so lovely," says 'Newbie', adjusting Rinty's new blue jacket. "He was walking up the road by our house. He was so thin I just had to take him in."

Our friend, Anne, had won the bet and was enjoying the cool beer we bought her, smiling rather smugly.

"You are just as bad as she is," I said.

"Yes, and that's why I won the bet. I can sniff these people out from a mile away."

She slid the glass of beer towards me.

"No time to drink that, I have dogs to walk."

Anne and her husband arrived in Spain a few years after we did. They brought their large dog, Peppie, with them. He accepted his new life in Spain, enjoying the new smells, new people, and sunshine. The only thing he didn't care for were the Spanish dogs.

During that first year, Anne saw a little Podenco (small hunting dog) living on the streets. Anne could tell that she had given birth a few times and needed care. Every day Anne would leave the little dog (now named Cassie) some food. It broke her heart that, because of Peppie, she couldn't take Cassie home.

At that time there were no rescue shelters or foster homes in which to place her. The one thing Anne could do was have her spayed. She and Cassie stayed in a B&B overnight and the operation was done the next day. A Spanish neighbour let Cassie stay with her, to recover, but they couldn't keep her for long. They already had dogs.

It was a heartbreaking situation but Anne could not bring another dog into their tiny home. Peppie had to come first. Two years had passed since Anne fell in love with this little stray and, when her dear Peppie died, Cassie had a home. Life was good for the couple. Cassie filled the hole that Peppie had left and all was well. Then sadly, Anne's beloved husband passed away.

A month later Anne spotted a friendly Bodeguera (similar to a Jack Russell) walking on the streets. The dog tried hard to make friends with people as they walked by, or as they sat outside a bar for coffee. I believe the dog was looking for one special person.

One hot afternoon, while the town was having its siesta, Anne walked Cassie along the streets, keeping to the shade. It was the only time she could walk without bumping into people who, of course, offered heartfelt condolences. But sometimes it was too much. Anne needed to walk in peace and deal with her grief in the best way that she could. She wanted to walk quietly with her dog.

There was the Bodeguera, lying in the shade outside a bar. Anne said, "Hello," and the dog followed her home, waited for the front door to be unlocked, and walked into the house as if she owned the place. Anne knew Lia was meant to be with her. Maybe the angels sent her, who knows, but the three lived in happy harmony, giving comfort to each other and making each other smile again.

A small dog rescue was started, just outside the town. It had very little funding but lots of heart. The English and Spanish stepped up to help feed, foster and adopt the many dogs that *La Huella Verde* rescued from the streets.

After the hunting season, they were overwhelmed with Podencos and Galgos, all needing feeding and fostering. They also needed funds to re-home the dogs, either locally or abroad. On their website a photo popped up of a Podenco Meneto, needing urgent fostering. She was housed with very big dogs and space was fast running out. They named her Kiara.

"I'm off to look at this Kiara dog, I might be able to foster her," Anne told me, as we drank coffee at the bar.

"You are going to foster?"

"Yes, I may foster. I can't take on another dog but I can help out for a few weeks. It's only for a few weeks."

She kept repeating 'few weeks' and I knew she was actually trying to convince herself. Sure enough, as I sat supping coffee with friends and frantically downloading podcasts, Anne walked across the Plaza with three dogs on leads.

"She is doing very well," she called out to us, on her way to her house. "She is house-trained and she will make a good companion."

We waved, smiling that smile. It would be just a matter of days now.

"I really can't have another dog in my tiny house," she said, trying to convince her audience on the second week of walking past the bar.

"It's done," we all agreed.

It was her Spanish neighbour who clinched it.

"I see you have another dog, Anne."

"Oh no," she replied. "I'm just fostering this one."

The Spaniard met her eyes.

"You have another dog, Anne."

She looked down at Kiara, and Kiara looked at her.

"Yes, you're right. I have another dog."

And that is how the magic happens. Animals find us. It's no use resisting.

"Diane, I need to steam Julio," said Antonio, phoning early in the morning.

"What's happened?"

"I didn't want to say it before but he's very ill. I can't clear his chest infection, the antibiotics haven't worked."

We finished milking and Pete dropped me off at the top of the track that lead to the *molino*. Antonio drove up to fetch me in the Land Rover.

"I have three flasks of hot water, eucalyptus and olbas oil," I told him.

"He is very bad, Diane, very bad."

I was shocked to see how much weight the big boy had lost. We set to with a bowl of steaming hot water laced with oils. Antonio covered his head in a sheet and cradled him in his arms, as dear Julio breathed in the steam.

"I am coming back early to Las Vicarias," he said, as he rocked Julio back and forth. "A storm is forecast and I want Julio home."

The following day, Pete helped move all the feed troughs and equipment into the trailer. Chickens and tiny babies were piled up in the tractor cab.

"Are you going to bring Julio back in the Land Rover later?" I asked.

"No, he will walk with me. I will walk slowly, but he will walk home."

Antonio knew that it was over and that this would be the last time his boy, Julio, could walk with the herd. He wanted to give him the respect and dignity he deserved. He also wanted to walk with his friend one last time.

Julio died the following day.

19

Carmen

We have an hour, maybe an hour and a half of grazing time left before heading home. The little 'biting bastards' are now out in full force. The mozzie spray spluttered the last of its death-juice way back in the cane tunnel.

I now resort to Bavarian Beer Dancing by slapping my thighs, hopping and swishing my arms around my head. The goats take little notice as they, too, tackle the pesky insects. They choose a head banging method. Perhaps 'Metallica' is playing in their collective consciousness.

Chinni halts the herd as they approach Antonio's sheds. She turns to wait for instructions. To be accurate, she turns and waits patiently for the panting and puffing human to catch up.

"Okay Chinni, this is the plan," I say, still trying to catch my breath. "I'll walk them up the track for a bit and you…"

She doesn't bother to wait for me to finish explaining. As usual, she has already worked out our next move. Chinni crosses the small *arroyo* and waits for me to walk up the track to higher ground. Her plan is to keep parallel with the herd and prevent them crossing over the *arroyo*. I have the easy job, pottering along the pot-holed track. It is time to check in with Pete.

"Hello, hello, can you hear me?" I say loudly into the phone.

"Yes, loud and clear. You must be up by the top sheds."

"Can you see us?"

"No, but Carmen is looking that way. She won't settle until you get back. I'll let her out into the olive paddock when I see you coming down the track for home. That'll put her mind at rest if you haven't fallen over. You haven't fallen over have you?"

"No, I haven't, but the day isn't done yet."

I fall over most days. I usually blame my boots.

It had been a drizzly, misty, dank morning and I really hoped it would clear up before walking the girls. We had fired up the wood burner early to dry our clothes and have a large pot of water heating. Our gas cylinder for the cooker was getting very low and our milk cheque would not arrive for another three days. Money was tight.

It was my turn to have new boots and the girls needed more mineral blocks. After a quick calculation we decided the only way to make it through another month was to have vegetable stew every night. With dumplings and bread to fill us up, we could survive.

Antonio had phoned to instruct me to be at his sheds one hour earlier than usual.

"There's rain coming later this afternoon so we'll be up on the hills behind your house," he said. "Oh, and don't wear that orange jacket. Put the green cape on."

My heart sank, remembering the last walk over this particular hill.

My brother-in-law had given me a wonderful bright orange postman's jacket. Wearing this in rainy conditions gave me comfort. If I fell, Peter could always find me and if I really fell, helicopters would be able to pick out my battered body.

Antonio's orders meant that we were going to walk illegally on someone else's land using the mist for cover. We had done this before. The huge hill and surrounding land is not grazed by sheep, cattle or goats. It is left wild, providing good cover for partridges, wild boar and hunters. The wild mountain goats may spend a few nights there, but they are wise enough to move on before hunting season begins.

It was the year of the rains. Weather fronts kept on rolling in, one after the other, for nearly three months. The river was impassable.

We kept the goats grazing on the hills and on the land that Antonio owned, opposite his sheds. After two weeks the tracks had become muddy and unstable and the goats were scratching for food.

"Right, I have a plan," said Antonio.

"And your plan is?"

"At six o'clock, we go over the big hill by your house."

"We can't do that. We'll get caught. And why wait until six o'clock?"

"Lady Dee, the goats are hungry, and so we do what we have to do to feed them. The ranger finishes work at six o'clock so we'll be safe."

And so for nearly three months we guided the two herds up the huge hill and they fed well on herbs, bracken and bushes. Antonio led the way, checking that all was clear in front.

The dogs walked in a straight line behind the herd, never once tempted to dash into a bush and flush out a skulking partridge. They knew to keep close and keep quiet. The rains kept coming and I was worried that the ranger would spot the hoofprints.

"Don't worry," Antonio said confidently, "he won't climb all the way up here in this weather."

Oh, but he did.

The rains had slowed to a light drizzle. The goats were now pretty fed up with the same routine. At the appointed time, Antonio led the miserable herds up onto the neighbour's hills, with the dogs and a tired English woman reluctantly following.

We climbed through the dense bushes, slowly gaining height. Monty kept close to my side, ready to drag me back to my feet if I tripped over roots, stones or my shoelaces. Suddenly the big boy growled. I stopped, quickly pulled out his lead from my huge pocket and clipped it on him.

Antonio was way ahead of me and I couldn't work out why Monty had suddenly gone onto high alert. A second later a ranger leapt out from behind a bush, waving his arms, and the goats scattered. I jogged up to Antonio, keeping a firm grip on Monty's lead, the ranger on my heels.

"Get your goats off this land, NOW!" he bellowed into Antonio's face.

Antonio put on his best boyish smile and cocked his head to one side.

"Good evening, Juan," he said. "The goats got away from me but no harm done, eh?"

"Got away from you!" spluttered the ranger. "Got away from you every day for a week, more like. I can see the hoofprints!"

Antonio turned to me and gave me a sly wink.

"Ah well, no harm done, Juan," he said.

"You bloody goatherders think you can get away with anything," he shouted. "Get off this land now."

"Okay, okay," said Antonio, before repeating, "no harm done."

I had heard enough. Antonio was keeping his temper but the lid had come off mine. I walked up to the red-faced little man with Monty standing close beside me. It's always a good idea to have an edge in tricky situations. Especially when you're in the wrong, but I didn't let that stop me.

Antonio dashed to the side of the ranger. I'm not sure if his instinct was to protect the man from the explosion that he knew was coming or to protect me from the 'jobs-worth' toad. We were in the wrong, and Antonio didn't want 'Clint Eastwood' appearing with a Magnum 44 and asking Juan to 'make his day'.

I took a step forward and invaded the poor man's space. He took one step back. I waited, curious to see which character would now take me over and deal with this unpleasant situation. It was dear Margot Leadbetter from the BBC comedy sitcom, *The Good Life*.

"You, whatever your name is, telephone your boss immediately. I wish to talk with him."

I was hoping my clipped posh accent translated into Andaluz. Antonio's eyes became wide and he mouthed the word 'no'. I ignored him.

"I am not phoning the boss. He will not speak to you. You are trespassing on his land!"

"He will speak to me," I said, my eyes narrowing, "because I'm his neighbour."

The little man's face contorted in an effort to remain calm. He was unsure, at this point, if I was bluffing or not.

"Being a neighbour makes no difference. You're on private property. Now get off this land."

He was regaining his composure and going on the attack again. Antonio shuffled sideways and indicated with a slight move of his head that we should bugger off quickly. But I was not finished, and neither was Margot.

"You refuse to telephone the owner of this land. Therefore you speak for him, yes?"

"Yes, I do."

"Let us be clear," I said, sounding like a dodgy politician. "You informed the owner about the damage the rains have caused. The worst rains in over sixty years, yes?"

"*Claro*, of course, he is aware."

"So… You're saying that the owner refuses to help a fellow neighbour in need by not allowing one hour of grazing on his many hectares of land," I said, dramatically waving my arm around. "That, sir, is not the Andaluz way. People in the *campo* help their neighbours. Please inform the owner that my article pointing this out will be appearing in two different newspapers in the coming weeks."

I turned and walked away, leaving the poor man open-mouthed. My only hope was that my Margot Leadbetter voice overcame my terrible Spanish. Mind you, the language seems a lot easier to speak when one is either drunk or angry. Monty nudged my leg and Antonio said nothing. When we finally arrived at the bottom of the hill I waited for some sort of praise for my outburst.

"Oh well, we got nearly three months of grazing out of it, so it ended well."

Silently I thanked Margot for stepping in to help today. It was not to be the last time.

At midday the valley was still hidden in mist. I needed to be in full camouflage gear to take the girls up the track to Antonio's by 1 pm.

Chinni had been running a temperature and so she was staying at home. Fliss (I named her in honour of my daughter) had cut her teat so walking through dense undergrowth was not a good idea. With Coco's early signs of dementia, it would be foolish to take her out in this weather. Mikki, Gerona and Ruby would also stay at home to keep her company. Monty and Paz were both sleeping by the fire, breathing in the smell of chicken soup that was simmering on the wood burner.

"The dogs can stay at home too," I told Pete. "They deserve a day off."

I bloody deserved a day off too, but such is the life of a lady goatherder.

The girls and I set off up the narrow track to Antonio's. Carmen, my darling sheep, led the way. The mist disorientated me and I couldn't work out where the edge of the path lay. The drop had A&E written all over it and so I fixed my eyes on Carmen's white rump. She guided me and the girls to the sheds.

"At last you're here."

"Are you sure this is a good idea?"

"Yes, of course it is a good idea. We only have two hours before heavy rain comes in so we'll keep low by the tracks. Don't forget, no talking. Your voice will carry in this weather."

We zig-zagged along the goat paths and yes, it was true, sound did carry further and was amplified in the mist. The goats began farting and I got the giggles. Carmen remained in front of me, allowing me to concentrate on staying on my own two feet and not veer off the path. After an hour, the mist began to lift and the rain began to fall.

Another hour passed and the wind got up before God really turned on the taps. In high winds and torrential rain, the goats ran past me, racing to get to Antonio's dry sheds. I tried to follow but couldn't see a thing through my glasses.

Stumbling down the track, I shouted to my girls. I had to get lower to direct my goats not to follow Antonio's herd. This was usually Chinni's job but now it was up to me. I stopped blindly jogging along the path to search in my pocket for loo paper to clean my glasses. It was then that the ground fell away, taking me with it.

Rocks, mud and a middle-aged woman slid down the hill. It happened so fast. I flung my arms out, trying to find a bush or boulder to grab to slow myself down. Eventually, my rucksack hooked itself onto a tree root nearly dislocating my shoulder in the process.

I crawled to my knees and lifted my head to the sky, letting the rain wash away the mud from my glasses. I knew most of my goats would now be with Antonio, warm in his sheds and eating his food. It would take Pete and me at least an hour or more to separate them, and to then coax them back home in the fading light.

I looked up the hill to the place where I should have been stationed and there she was, a white beacon instructing the girls to turn right towards our farm. I tried to stand, but my feet slipped from under me and my bum hit the ground. There was no point in calling out to Carmen. I just watched, and imagined her 'Lady Bracknell' voice commanding the goats to go home.

I searched my pockets for more loo paper. When I looked up, Carmen was gone. I began crawling a little further down the hill to find more solid ground. I felt useless and pitiful, and the tears began to drip down my mud-splattered face. I looked up again to get my bearings and there, trotting up the path towards me, was Carmen.

"Carmen, you came back!" I sobbed.

"Get up, you stupid woman and follow me."

Her eyes met mine.

"Thank you Carmen," I sobbed even louder, before slowly getting to my feet.

I, once again, followed her large white rump back to the farm. I could hear Pete calling for both of us.

"I'm here. Carmen came back for me," I said.

Peter stared at the creature that was crying and caked in mud. He turned and ushered Carmen into a pen, then rushed away to fetch her food, leaving me dripping in the shed. Chinni was standing in the next pen and gave me a comforting look. At least I *thought* it was a comforting look. Maybe it was pity.

Carmen

"Are all the goats here, Pete?"

"Yep, I've done a head count. Carmen ran them all into the paddock before taking off at the speed of a fat sheep, back up the track. I thought that you still had goats stuck up there until I did a head count."

"No, Peter, it was a bloody landslide but I'm fine," I sniffed.

With as much dignity as a creature from a mud swamp could muster, I went indoors to face Monty and Paz, before showering in a freezing cold bathroom. Later, over stew and bread, we went over the afternoon's events.

We came to the conclusion that people would not believe how this sheep was far more capable of dealing with a crisis than the humans she lives with. Of course, this was not the first time that Carmen had come to the rescue.

Spring had arrived. The river was passable and the sun had come out. The herd wanted to cross, to eat the lush grass on the other side. We'd had some late births and Pete was enjoying having the babies 'help' him clean the stables.

They ran in and out, twirling and skipping, distracting Peter from his shit-shovelling duties. When I leave with the goats, all the babies were rounded up and locked in pens until the herd was out of sight. Then they were let out to play again.

This particular afternoon, the goats ran to the river, found the stepping stones to cross and put their heads down to graze on the other side.

Jogging across the field to catch up, I noticed with horror that two of Cassie's kids had escaped. With any other goat I wouldn't have been overly concerned. But Cassie loves the water and will walk, belly deep, to munch on the tastiest foliage hanging low on the river bank.

Luck was with me. Mariposa had the hump and decided to take it out on Cassie. Just as Cassie was about to wade into the river, her babies hot on her heels, Mariposa turned on her and started a fight. This gave me enough time to remove a lead rope from my rucksack and catch Cassie.

I phoned Peter but there was no signal. He was obviously in the stable playing chase with the other babies. My brain got into gear. I sent Paz across the river to hold the herd before carefully leading Cassie to the stepping stones. The babies duly followed with Monty positioning himself behind them.

Sending up a silent prayer, I ran Cassie across the river and the babies jumped from stone to stone, following their mother. Cassie still hadn't cottoned on that her children were following her and dashed off to graze, leaving her tired, hot and scared kids in the care of Monty. The babies crawled into the shade of a tree, Monty staying close.

I phoned Peter every half hour but he didn't answer. He must have had his blasted headphones on, listening to music. I needed him to get to the river and help get the babies across with their mother, at exactly the same spot. If the babies crossed upriver, where the water was deeper, the weeds below the surface could easily wrap around their legs.

My only option was to catch Cassie, who only allows me to touch her when she is giving birth or being milked. I decided to try Antonio's trick of hiding in between the herd, before leaping out with the speed of a cobra to grab her back leg.

Everything is in the timing and at the precise moment that I was about to execute my Bruce Lee move, Pete dished out the goat's dinner into the feed troughs. Fat Pat was the first to hear the sound of grain falling into the troughs and made a dash for the stepping stones. The rest of the herd followed, except Cassie, who jumped into the river and was first on the other side.

I watched open-mouthed, as she galloped back to the sheds to be first in line at the dinner table. Paz took off with the herd to make sure that all the goats were safely in the paddock, leaving myself, Monty and the two kids, who had now woken up. I was too slow trying to catch them, so looked at Monty for inspiration.

"Bloody hell Monty, now what do we do?"

I needed a plan. Monty seemed to be temporarily baffled.

"Okay," I said. "I'll get them to follow me to the crossing, while you push them from behind."

Miraculously they followed, but on reaching the last stone they panicked and ran back through Monty's legs. We both said 'bugger' at the same time, as we now had babies screaming on one side of the river and us on the other. I phoned Peter again and at last, he answered.

"Get Cassie to the river, NOW!" I said, and ended the call.

I wrestled with my double knotted laces to remove my boots, in case I needed to get into the river and rescue the kids if they jumped in. Then the cavalry arrived. Carmen.

She had raced across the field, waded into the river, climbed the bank and shooed the kids along to the stepping stones. I quickly turned on my phone to film the rescue. Peter arrived, dragging Cassie behind him.

It suddenly dawned on her that these were her own missing babies. She called to them as Carmen pushed them across the last of the stepping stones. They ran to their mother. Carmen briskly walked past me muttering, "idiot" under her breath. Pete and I stared at each other.

"Diane, I can't believe that just happened," he said. "Did that just happen?"

We slowly walked back to the farm and pondered events over a glass of wine.

The hill opposite the farm is also privately owned. They graze a handful of Retinta cattle on it. These are huge cows, red, with long pointed horns. As with most animals, the grass is always greener on the other side of the fence and, in their case, it's true.

One cow finds a chink in the fence and pops over to the river to graze, with the rest of the herd hot on her heels. We don't make a fuss over this intrusion onto our land. Instead, we simply graze our girls on their hillside during the late afternoon. A good deal, I think, and no one is any the wiser.

It had been a dry spring and by the summer, all reserved eating grounds were getting sparse. Antonio had moved his herd to his brother's farm to look for grazing, leaving the river beds to me. The cows and the goats had a great routine.

Every evening, the cows climbed down their narrow path to a hole in the broken fence, hopped over, and crossed the river to graze on our land. We waited until they settled before sneaking past them onto their hill, to graze on the herbs. All went swimmingly well until one particular evening, just as darkness was about to fall.

I called the girls down from the hill to cross the river and head for home via a small hunters' gate, but only half the herd turned up. Normally I would send Paz up to investigate but she had had a nasty problem with a grass seed and her foot was in a poultice. I called and called, but could see no rustling in the high bushes. I phoned Pete.

"I've lost half the herd so I'm bringing this lot in. Get the torches."

"Shit Diane, how could you…"

"No time to argue. Open the gate and I'll be there in five minutes."

Peter met me at the gate, torches in hand. We did a quick check. Both of the sheep were back as were the special-needs, Coco, Mikki and Gerona. Then my heart sank. The older, sensible ones like Welfi, Milly, Hildy, Alice, Pat and, of course, Chinni, were in the paddock.

Damn it. Most of the young idiots, as well as Willow the trouble-maker, were lost high on the hill and the light was fading very fast. We ran across the river and onto the small flat ground, under the crag. Pete immediately started climbing to the left and I jogged to the right, shining my torch into the bushes. I called quietly and heard Pete swear loudly. It was time to make the phone call.

"Antonio, half the herd is lost on the hill and it's almost dark, what do I do?"

This was the umpteenth time that I'd phoned him to ask a ridiculous question, expecting him to come up with a solution.

"Leave them there. Keep the little gate open all night and they'll come home at first light," he said calmly.

"No, no, no! What about stray dogs, wild boar and vampires? I can't do that!"

"Okay, just go and get Carmen."

Why didn't I think of that? I jogged back to the paddock to find Carmen waiting for me at the gate and, as I lifted the latch, she barged passed me, muttering something I couldn't quite catch.

Unlike goats, sheep are not afraid of the dark and so I found myself, yet again, following a large white rump into the moonless *campo*. My torch had little battery left and my night vision was nil.

"Carmen is here, Peter," I called out to the hill.

The big white sheep stood in the small clearing at the foot of the hill. She raised her head, sniffed and then stomped her foot.

"Baaaaa!" she cried.

Slowly the goats appeared. As soon as they saw Carmen they rushed down the hill and stood by her. Peter then appeared dazed and grazed.

"Bloody goats," he said. "I've climbed through these sodding bushes calling for them. Just one word from Carmen and they all come running. What does that say about us?"

Carmen didn't bother listening to her humans. She just turned and led the goats back home with us following behind, once again in debt to a big fat sheep.

How do we measure intelligence in an animal? Maybe we shouldn't. Maybe we should just accept that their understanding of the world is far greater than ours.

I do wonder what Carmen really thinks of me. She mutters 'idiot' most days when I trip over, get lost or fail to see a huge wild boar in a bush, even though she has loudly warned me by stamping her foot. She restores order to the chaos I create in a simple afternoon walk.

We had an invite for dinner with a friend and so our routine had to be altered for us to be scrubbed and changed in time. This meant the goats had to go out two hours earlier. However, we didn't need two hours to get ourselves ready. Past experience had taught us to plan ahead in case of surprises that may occur during a goat walk.

To save Peter from having to chop down olive branches to feed the sheep and special-needs girls, I decided to take everyone out but to keep close to home. The sheep could take shade under the poplar trees and the girls with disabilities could cope in the heat, if we didn't walk too far.

All the girls settled down and I joined the sheep. Some of the goats walked along the river bank whilst others dived deep into the fern and munched. The pressing decision for me that afternoon was whether or not to remove my chipped nail varnish, or just paint over the cracks.

I closed my eyes for a few minutes, (at least I thought it was only a few minutes) before being bitten by a pesky horse fly. Swearing loudly I slapped my leg, waking up a sheep in the process. She was not amused. Never mind, it was time to slowly move the goats downriver for the last hour.

I scanned the river bank and saw Chinni, Mikki and Gerona, their heads down, enjoying the river foliage. I blinked and my brain started to catch up. The rest of the herd had disappeared.

"Chinni, where are the girls?" I shouted.

Chinni looked up. Her brain was working much faster than mine and she immediately took off at a run to a gap in the fence, leading for my neighbour's hill. I had to move fast and run downriver to head them off at the tiny hunters' gate before they all buggered off out of sight. Carmen and Loretta were both up and following me downriver.

"I'm cutting them off at the gate," I shouted back to Carmen, hoping she would approve of my quick thinking.

By now, Chinni should have found the girls and, with luck, guided them down to the small clearing where I would soon be waiting.

"There they are, Carmen," I said, pointing at moving bushes halfway up the hill.

It was then that I remembered my special-needs goats. I had left them grazing two river crossings away. I phoned Peter, told him what had happened and to go pick them up.

"Don't let the goats get past you Diane," he bellowed. "Get Paz to bring them down to the gate. We are not going to be late for dinner. Who have you got with you?"

"Loretta and…" I paused. "I can't see Carmen, but she was with me."

I could feel the tension brewing at the end of the phone and so I thought it best to keep my mouth shut. If I said out loud the words that were forming in my mind, we would arrive at our friend's house in the stony silence of a couple who have just had a huge row in the car. No smiles can hide it.

"It's fine," I said calmly. "I'm sending Paz up now and Carmen won't be far away.

"Okay. I'm off to check the olive grove and let's hope the girls haven't tried to cross upriver in the deep bit." He abruptly cut the call.

Chinni was leading the herd down and Paz was ready to move fast should any make a break to the right. It was time to look for Carmen.

I walked towards the river and there she was, walking towards me with the three old girls following her. As soon as she saw Chinni was in control of the herd she must have doubled back, crossed the river twice, found the girls and led them back to me. I phoned Pete. She had saved the day again.

I called up to Chinni.

"Take 'em home, Chinni, take 'em home."

Carmen looked at me, as I smiled and gushed at her for being such a wonderful friend. I hoped she understood how much she meant to me.

She met my eyes, and in her best 'Lady Bracknell' voice said, "Idiot!"

20

Donkeys and Horses

Chinni turns away from the herd and begins to slowly guide them towards the last hill's grazing before heading down the track for home. It's about forty-five minutes before dusk and that magical moment when the valley is bathed in gold. The girls quietly file past me, following Chinni, who is slowly climbing high and searching for herbs.

When I had reached the great age of one, Sandra pulled me from our mum's clutches, placed me in front of her saddle and off we went. She even trotted over poles on the ground. I squealed and Dad panicked, trying to drag me from the saddle. I held tight onto the pony's mane.

As I grew so did my imagination. The back of the sofa turned into Roy Rogers' horse, Trigger. A golden birch tree became Fury, the black stallion. I named my first bicycle, Champion, and my first horse, Rocky.

I was around eleven years old when Dad bought me a six-month old coloured Cob. For nearly thirty years we were together. It's only now that I realise that the animals that came into my life have one thing in common. They totally understand their human and accept that their human is a first-class twit.

The years passed and I had moved from Kent to Dorset. Rocky and I loved to ride the bridleways around Studland. It was a hot Sunday afternoon and I thought it perfect to explore the heathland.

Smothering Rocky and myself in fly repellant, I climbed onto him, wearing shorts and plimsolls, hoping to catch a tan. I rode bareback so as not to pinch my legs on the stirrup leathers.

The heathland was very quiet at this time of the day. Most sensible people were on the beach. Rocky was not happy and I couldn't understand why. The fly repellant was working fine but he began to snort and jog along the narrow pathways.

His jogging awoke my bladder and I needed to find a place to pee. I dismounted and this alarmed Rocky even more. I couldn't figure out what was the matter with him.

"Okay, we'll go back home, Rock. I just need to find a place to pee."

I realised that, with no convenient bush to hand, I would just have to 'go' using Rocky as cover. The next moment Rocky pushed me to his left before turning into a crazy, wild Mustang. His ears were flat back and his front legs stomped the ground. I thought he'd found a wasps' nest and, if not that, then I had no idea what the matter was with him.

And then I saw. Rock calmly stood back, revealing a snake, smashed to a pulp. My need to pee had vanished and I clambered up onto his back.

"Let's go home, Rock. Let's just go home."

He agreed and we headed back to the field.

Rocky was a true gentleman. He loved ladies and mares, but had a deep mistrust of men. No man had ever mistreated him but he just didn't trust them, especially flirty farriers.

A nervous giggle from me as a teenager would put Rocky into protection mode and the poor farrier would suddenly have a back leg lashing out at him.

One time, as I was putting a battery on a new line of electric fence wire, two young farmhands thought it a wheeze to grab my arm and see if the battery was working.

It was all done in good fun but I screamed, as they expected me to do, in anticipation of an electric shock. Rocky was grazing on the opposite side of the field and, hearing my cry, came galloping in with his ears back and baring his teeth.

The poor young boys ran for their lives and, thank the Lord, they made it back to the gate in time. My big white boy, his black splodges having long, long disappeared, spent his life looking after me. When his time came to leave this world, my heart was shattered. I was inconsolable.

Eight months passed and I was totally lost. For thirty years I had owned a horse. What on earth was I to do now? How should I fill this empty space in my life?

A friend suggested that I should look at two local foals, just born, one black and white, one bay. Six months later they came home to live with me. My youngest daughter fell in love with the piebald boy and we named him Beau. The big bay foal I named Hardy.

Beau grew to 14.2 hh, a handsome boy who loved my daughter. Hardy took his genes from his father, a Shire. He (Hardy) grew to 16.1 hh and was built like a tank. I worried he would be too much horse for me but after a few hairy moments in his training, he turned out to be one of the easiest horses I have ever ridden.

Years went by and the winters in Dorset seemed to become a problem. Flooded fields, mud, and the lack of local bridle paths made me wonder if the dream of one day moving to Spain could become a reality. Four years later the dream came true.

The horses arrived in Spain, perfectly happy after their four day journey. My vet, in England, assured me that they would handle the heat and he was right. Not only did they cope with the heat, they enjoyed eating the foreign food, cane leaves and the lush green foliage that grew by the side of the river. Hardy, who had a fear of puddles in England, now happily strolled in the river to cool his hooves.

Beau and Hardy

Although Hardy gave the appearance of being the horse in charge, it was always Beau that led them out to graze, keeping to a strict time-table. Hardy, like me, has no sense of direction, which is unheard of in a horse.

But now (maybe because all of his life he'd relied on Beau to guide him home) when the pair ducked under the electric tape to explore pastures new upriver, Beau's inner clock and compass would have them back in the stable waiting for breakfast at exactly 8.30 am.

They'd then rest until midday before going out for an hour in the blistering heat, returning to the stable for a snooze until 9 pm.

Wintertime was different and Beau would lead them out at 4 pm then back home at 8 pm for supper. I could set my watch by him.

The children came to visit when they could. My eldest daughter, Amelia, was now married and expecting her first baby. Pete's children, Rose and Arthur, were at university and college respectively and Fliss, my youngest, was working whilst going to college. She would come over every opportunity she had.

On arriving at the farm she would say hello to the dogs, and then us, before dashing off, head-collar in hand, to find Beau. Fliss rode him bareback across the river, cantering in the field, before returning back to the stable where the grooming would begin. Beau loved being reunited with his best friend.

I wanted Fliss to experience that golden moment, just before dusk, to be in the middle of the valley when the light changed. We tacked up the boys and did a little schooling in the paddock. To be honest, Fliss did the schooling as Hardy and I ambled around the field, bird watching. I saw the sky begin to change.

"Come into the big field, Fliss," I called.

Girl and pony walked to the middle of the field and within seconds, both were enveloped in gold. It was a moment I wished I had captured on camera. But the image remains locked in my memory forever.

Horsey people tend to find horsey people. Andy and Julie were horsey people. In truth, it was Julie who'd had horses throughout her life. Andy just went with the flow.

We met for coffee in the town to discuss Julie's hunt for a Spanish horse. Andy was figuring a way to rescue a donkey that was staked out on their land. This is the story of Jenny…

A gentleman from the town (we will call him OG, short for Old Git) grew vegetables on Andy and Julie's land. He would grow the veg and they could take as much as they needed at harvest time. They were finishing off building stables and it seemed like a good deal.

OG borrowed two mules from a neighbour, to plough and maintain the land, and all was going well until the neighbour sold the mules. OG then borrowed money from another neighbour to buy a large donkey to work the land.

Jenny arrived and she was not in good shape. Her front legs were swollen and her hooves were very overgrown. OG staked her out in the sun, tying one leg to a rough piece of rope and attached to a wooden stake. Julie couldn't understand why he didn't just put the donkey into the shade of the olive grove.

Grabbing her binoculars she looked more closely and saw that there was no water bucket. She waited for an hour to see if OG would appear with refreshment. She did not want to create problems or appear to be a pushy English woman. But, once the hour had passed, she'd had enough.

Filling a large container and grabbing a bucket, she set off with a wheelbarrow and walked across the field to Jenny. As she filled the bucket, OG stood up from his resting place in the olive grove and began to shout.

"Don't give her water! She only works when she is thirsty!"

Julie ran back to the house and told Andy. They waited until it was dark before taking more water and food over to Jenny. They needed a plan to save this donkey but they had to box clever.

OG owned her, even if he had bought her on borrowed money. By agreement he had planted vegetables on their land and therefore they couldn't just kidnap her. Nor did they want to call the police, it being a small town.

A week later, Andy saw that Jenny had fallen down a bank. He rushed across the field and found her in a terrible position. Unable to get to her feet, her tethered leg was pulled up at a horrible angle. He quickly cut the rope and phoned Julie who arrived ten minutes later. Laden with wet towels, she placed these on Jenny's head and body.

They called the local vet. Jenny was close to death. She could barely hold her head up to sip the water. When the vet arrived he rehydrated her and helped get her to her feet. Julie said she would pay the bill but explained that it wasn't their donkey.

"She will be by tonight," said Andy, as he slowly walked Jenny across the field to the stable.

In the early evening OG arrived, ready to do a bit of chain harrowing with Jenny. He was met by Julie. In true *Godfather* style, Julie made OG an offer he couldn't refuse.

The deal was that she would buy Jenny at full price, pay the vet bill and compensate him for half of the vegetables. But his time working on their land was now over.

She looked him in the eye and, in fluent Essex, said, "Now sod off, you little shit!"

Jenny could now enjoy retirement. It took a long time for the farrier to correct her deformed hooves. However, she was out of pain and now residing in a five-star hotel. She had rugs in the winter, thick straw in a warm stable at night, and a cool stable in the summer.

Andy doted on her. She lived for years, enjoying the love he gave her, but her hard life began to catch up with her. Getting up in the morning was becoming more and more difficult.

Pete, or another friend, Kevin, would dash down to help lift the old lady. But the day came when her body just said, 'no more'. She couldn't hold her weight and when Julie looked into her eyes, she knew the time had come. Julie had found a wonderful equine vet, Marina, based in Ronda, and made the call.

Marina arrived, a lovely young woman, who showed kindness and understanding at this sad time. She spoke gently to Jenny and was compassionate with Andy and Julie. We stood back to give the couple space to say goodbye. Andy held Jenny's head, talking gently to his friend as she slipped into that deep, sleep.

It was now time to make a move. The three ladies returned to the house to drink coffee and regain composure. The digger man had arrived and there was no need for Andy to stay now as the others would sort out Jenny. The men tried to get Andy to join us but he wouldn't leave her.

"She's my responsibility and I'll see this through," he said climbing onto his tractor, ready to move Jenny to her final resting place.

We ladies had a group hug, cried, and then hugged some more.

"My job is to save lives," said Marina. "When I can't, it hurts."

It was wonderful to meet such a kind vet and I hoped we would meet again under better circumstances. We did meet again a year later. The day my heart broke.

21

Take them home, Chinni...

Chinni is watching me from the top of the hill. I check my watch to find that we still have another twenty minutes before we head home.

I walk along the lower part of the hill to have a chat with my old faithfuls, Welfi, Sandra and Milly. They quietly graze with India and Isabelle, the late great Pepita's daughter.

Chinni probably recruited them long ago to keep an eye on me during our walks. Or maybe they just like having a good laugh when I get things wrong.

Antonio was back at his summer sheds at the *molino* and we had met up at the canyon. Once again he had lost his hoof-trimmers and needed to borrow mine. He had little time. Three of his girls had gone into labour and he did a quick turn around to get the herd back to the sheds before they gave birth.

My water was running low so I walked back with him to refill my bottle. Both herds took off, hoping to get an early supper. I was 'tail-end-Charlie' and it was my job to check that nobody had fallen asleep in the cane.

Suddenly I stopped in my tracks. I thought I'd heard a puppy crying. Being partially deaf I can hear high tones but hadn't a clue about the direction of the sound. Never fear, Welfi could. She had stopped in the river bed and looked up at the tall cliff. Following her gaze, I made out the shape of a puppy running up and down along the top of the cliff.

"Oh heavens, Welfi, it's going to fall! I have to rescue it!"

She turned and left me.

The cliff face had great white stones sticking out, forming a perfect climbing wall. The pup's cries were getting louder so I dumped my rucksack in the sand and began to climb, sensing I was being watched.

I slowly turned my head, hoping that Antonio had returned to provide support. But no, it was the gang. Welfi must have put out the call that 'Mother' had gone nuts again and five goats had settled down to watch the show.

I had seen people on the television racing up climbing walls. How hard could it be? Hands and feet found good solid stones and my climbing got quicker as the pup's whines got louder. My head and shoulders reached the top and thankfully, the pup came straight to me.

Grabbing it with one hand, I shoved the terrified creature inside my shirt. Getting up was the easy part, now I had to descend. The fourth stone that my left foot found started to move so I side-stepped it and found another. But that one came out too, spinning away to the bottom. When the stone that my right hand was gripping came out of the cliff, time stood still.

My brain was racing. I remembered Peter's advice: "If you're going to fall, control it the best you can." However, when he said it, I was fairly convinced that he wasn't sober.

I had no idea what he meant at the time but in that split second it became crystal clear. Directly below me were scattered rocks and boulders. I needed to hit the damp sand, a few feet beyond.

I turned and kicked away from the cliff, the sand rushing up to meet me. I held the pup tight to my chest with my right hand. As my feet touched the ground, I executed a rather spectacular triple roll and stood up.

The goats all stared at me and I stared back, waiting for a round of applause. Entertainment over, they all stood up and went to find the rest of the herd. The puppy was fine but my bra was now full of fleas. I finally caught up with Antonio and the girls at the mill.

"Where have you been? Penelope (Cruz) has just had a big girl," he said, beaming.

I told my tale and handed over the pup. I'm not sure what response I expected but, as usual, Antonio floored me.

"You're an idiot. What a stupid thing to do," he said, shaking his head.

"I had to save her and you'd left."

"Did you not wonder, Diane, how she got up there?"

"Of course I didn't," I said. "There was no time."

"Oh, I see. Well, by not thinking, you could have broken your back. That risk was better than thinking?"

"Okay, Maestro, what should I have done?"

"First," he said, smiling, "realise that she came from here. Second, walk up the river to the cane and see the path that leads to the top of the cliff. Third, walk up the path and call the puppy."

"Oh," was all I could muster.

"Chinni must've known you would do this," he said, still smiling, or it could've been a smirk. "She stood by the bank and wouldn't come to the mill."

"Oh," I repeated.

"She has faith that you think as she does." He was now on a roll. "She must be very disappointed that you haven't learnt anything from her."

"Yes," I said, now totally deflated.

Not wishing to see me dissolve into tears, or worse, bash my head on the eucalyptus tree in despair, he ushered me into the shed to see Penny's new daughter and to refill my water container.

"The jump was a good idea," he said quietly.

"Yes, it was, wasn't it?" I smiled again.

"Oh, and be on alert for Isabelle. She will give birth tonight or tomorrow."

"Righto!" I was still smiling.

I said goodbye to the puppy. Little did I know that in less than a month, she would become part of our 'family'.

Isabelle would normally have stayed home, in my estimation, three days from giving birth. But she became quite stressed if she was not allowed to walk with the herd.

The following day, as Antonio predicted, she was getting ready to go into labour, although it could still be hours away. I decided to stay close to home and let her out with the herd.

No sooner had I crossed our big field when I heard the distinctive, "bub, bub, bub," voice of a goat in labour. Sure enough, it came from Isabelle.

I called Pete, who was just about to clean out the horse stable, to come and pick her up.

"Okay, okay. I'm on my way now."

With collar and lead in hand, he caught Isabelle and led her back to the goat paddock. The last time she gave birth, Peter was alone with her and she presented him with a tricky situation. He was about to assist her delivery when he saw four front feet present. There was no time to phone me or Antonio.

He considered pushing one of the babies back inside but then two heads appeared and two kids fell to the floor. After a few seconds of rapid blinking, Pete lifted the kids up and let Isabelle clean the pair.

Two lots of afterbirth came away, the babies were feeding and mum was happy. With the job done, Pete dashed to the fridge for a cool beer.

About an hour into our walk the phone rang and my day turned into a nightmare.

"Are you close?" asked Pete.

"Yes, quite close. Has Isabelle got a problem?"

"It's not Isabelle, Diane. It's Beau. He's breathing hard and sweating."

These symptoms are a horse owner's dread. It's the 'C' word.

Colic.

"Call Julie and get her to phone Marina. Tell her it's colic. I'm coming in now, just leave the gate open." My heart was pounding.

Paz rounded up the goats fast, sensing the urgency, and together we pushed them back into their paddock. I found Peter attending to Isabelle's babies.

"Julie and Andy are on their way. Andy will go back and wait for the vet at the top of the track, to guide her down."

Although he knew that this was serious, he thought the vet would quickly sort it. I ran to the stable and found Beau breathing hard. I pressed my head to his tummy but could hear no movement. Leaving Hardy in the paddock, I coaxed Beau into the big field, praying to all that was good in the universe to help him.

Julie arrived and Andy went straight back to meet the vet. The light was now fading fast as Julie and I began a conversation that was full of half-truths, but the intention was to give hope.

"What do you think Marina will do first?" I asked, knowing the answer.

"Drench him Diane, and check for a blockage. She will sedate him first, of course."

We both knew that we were talking to each other like beginners, and we both knew that this was bad. Julie was trying to protect me, while I didn't want to let my daughter down by allowing negative thoughts to enter my brain.

I saw Beau's eyes widen. I smelt his breath and knew it was 'game over'. His heart was giving out. Out of the corner of my eye I could see lights coming down the track.

"She's coming Diane, she's coming!" shouted Peter.

Andy was guiding the vet as fast as he could along our narrow track, while Julie was now watching Beau as intently as I was.

"Step back, Diane, NOW!" she ordered.

It all happened at once. Marina's car burst into the field as Beau went down.

"No, no, no!" shouted Marina as she leapt out of her car, syringe in hand.

I held his head as Marina injected him.

I looked up at Peter who was standing, mouth open, in total shock. He had never witnessed an animal of this size go down. He had faith that we could save him, but this was so quick. I stroked my beautiful boy's head, held him and kissed him. All voices around me disappeared. It was just me and him.

"Diane, Diane. Marina is going now," said Peter.

I came out of this odd trance, walked up to the vet and we embraced. She understood that I could say nothing. With my hug I conveyed my thanks to her for her quick response.

Andy and Pete found a tarpaulin and placed it over Beau's body. There were phone calls to make. Andy called the digger man while I found a quiet spot in the olive grove to make the call to Felicity. When everyone had gone home, I made myself a coffee.

"Diane, come to bed. You need to get some sleep," said Peter.

"Okay, I'll come in a bit," I lied.

I finished my coffee and walked back to Beau. Hardy was there. I had let him out of the paddock and left him alone to give him time to take in what had happened. I sat down next to Beau and quietly talked to Hardy but human words were not needed.

Hardy and I stayed together next to Beau, both lost in our own thoughts. I recalled that first year we came to Spain, Felicity on Beau, standing close to the spot where he now lay, both bathed in that beautiful golden light just before dusk.

Dawn had arrived and it was time to milk the goats. I stood and stroked Hardy.

"Come and have breakfast early today, son," I said.

My innocent big 'tank' of a horse looked at me and then at Beau. It was not time for breakfast. He walked towards the river, still looking for his friend.

Eight months had passed since losing Beau. Hardy was coping by keeping to the same routine that Beau had set, but I had to find him a companion. At twenty years old, Hardy had, God willing, many years ahead of him and he was not going to spend them alone.

Winter was here, and it was not a good time to introduce a new horse to the farm. Yes, there was lots of food but the constant worry of storms, and the need to bring horses in fast, may be difficult with a horse that was new to my voice. My main concern was finding the right companion. How would I judge if a new horse would be the right personality for Hardy to bond with?

A storm was approaching fast. Antonio and I were on the hill behind my house. Hardy was on the other side of the river and Pete was in town.

"I've got to go and get Hardy across the river," I told Antonio.

"Don't panic, Diane," he said. "He will cross soon. He knows the river after all these years."

"No, he won't. It's not time for him to cross."

Antonio looked at me, bemused.

"Antonio, he keeps to a set time-table. He will only change it if I catch him and bring him in."

Another clap of thunder echoed through the valley and I could see the river starting to pick up speed.

"I'm going to go and get him so don't let my goats see which way I've gone," I said.

"Okay, I'll move them round the corner," he said, and started to whistle the herds.

I waited for a few minutes until the herd rounded the corner and was out of sight. It took me no time to get to the bottom of the hill, sliding down the bank into the adjoining olive grove.

Carmen, realising that something was up, came with me. Legging it through the gate and into the feed room I grabbed a bucket, (putting a handful of pony nuts into it, so that it would rattle) before sprinting into the field. Hardy seemed oblivious of the danger and just carried on munching.

"Hardy," I yelled, at the top of my voice. "Get across, NOW!"

He looked up, to see me and a fat sheep bellowing at him.

Thank the Lord he came, the rattling bucket and Carmen's presence clinching it. The river was now belly high and moving very fast but he just ploughed in, never faltering in his stride. His 16.1 hh height and his 'Shire' bulk saved him, as it would years later when he was caught in a flash flood and nearly drowned.

Thunder crashed around us. Carmen took off, but not towards the horse paddock. She jogged to the small paddock directly in front of the house. Peter had arrived home and ran to open the gate only to see a fat sheep, a horse and a wife running towards him.

"Hardy is staying here, tonight," I told him.

"But, he won't have any shelter," said Peter.

"No, but he can see and hear us in the house. Plus, Carmen made the decision.

"Right... Okay then," he muttered. "I'll dish out the dinner for the goats and go and find them."

Chinni, Paz and Monty had already brought the girls home and they were all in the paddock, waiting to be let into the stable. The thunder got louder, and lightning lit up the sky. I knew Hardy was nervous, but Beau had always been there to reassure him. Now, he only had me. The rain came and I stood outside with my big boy, holding up his bucket of food for him.

It'll be okay, Hardy. I'll find you a friend," I told him. But he didn't understand. He already had a friend, but he couldn't find him. Beau had gone.

Spring came early, and I wanted Hardy to have a vet check him over and rasp his teeth. Marina came, and Hardy was on his best behaviour, well, he was after she'd administered a sedative. I told Marina how I needed to find a companion for Hardy and that I had contacted rescue sites, but the horses that were available were too young. I needed an older horse.

"I'll keep a look out for you, Diane," she said.

A week later she phoned.

"I have the perfect horse for Hardy," she said. "Can you meet me in Ronda tomorrow, at 1 pm? I'll take you to see him."

After writing down the directions, I phoned Eileen.

"Are you free for a road trip tomorrow?"

"Oh hell, what mess are you in now?" she said.

"No mess. We're going to see a horse."

"Okay, I'm in. I suppose you want me to drive?"

"Do you trust me to get us to Ronda in one piece?" I said, knowing the answer.

"I'll pick you up at 12."

We arrived at the hotel meeting place and Marina found us, five minutes later.

"He is an old boy and very, very skinny," she said.

"Has he been mistreated?" I asked.

"No, I've known this boy for a long time and he was very much loved, but he's now in quite a tricky situation," she said.

I waited for further information, but none was forthcoming.

"Are there any other problems?"

"He's very difficult to catch," she said, quickly gathering up her car keys.

We drove off, following Marina closely along the winding tracks before finally stopping outside a beautiful *cortijo* (farmhouse), which was surrounded by vineyards. We were met at the gate by three gentlemen who led us in silence to a large post and railed paddock.

Two very fat 'warm-bloods' were munching hay close to the stable block and behind them, standing in the corner of the paddock, was a skeleton. Marina instructed the farm hands to catch the horse, leaving Eileen and me to study the poor old boy.

"Bloody hell, Diane, he's practically dead," said Eileen.

"Mmm," I replied.

I could see that he was in very bad shape and that one eye was closed up. But there was something…

The men went in to catch him and that 'something' became clear. He moved with such grace and beauty that my eyes misted over, just watching him.

"Look Eileen, look," I said softly.

"Yeah well, from the chest down he looks like a horse. But let's face it, Diane, he's dead from the neck up."

She had a point.

The men had no luck catching him, and the horse was sweating and coughing.

"Let's give him a rest, please," I said.

Happy to return to their cans of beer, the men walked back to the stable block. Marina came over to us, looking very concerned.

"What's his name?" I asked.

"His previous owner named him Bailey."

It was time to put away the dozy, blonde Englishwoman and take over.

"Marina, get those other two horses stabled and make up a feed bucket for me. Put it by the gate."

Marina left to sort out the other horses, and I climbed into the paddock.

"What are you doing, Diane?" asked Eileen. "Don't go getting kicked in the head. Mind you, we are close to the hospital so carry on."

"I'm going for a chat with Bailey."

Eileen lit a cigarette and leant over the paddock rail to watch her friend, yet again, make a fool of herself.

I'm not a brilliant rider, I never have been. But I can talk 'horse'. I figured that if I could just have a talk with Bailey, then all would be well. I took deep breaths, cleared my head of thoughts and concentrated on the paddock floor. Slowly, I walked sideways into the middle, my eyes never leaving the dusty ground.

"He's not looking at you," Eileen called out.

A careful sideways look towards Bailey told me that he was, indeed, looking at me. One ear had locked on. After more deep breaths I began to slowly walk in circles, dropping my shoulder as I turned. I waited and took more deep breaths, my eyes still fixed to the ground. I repeated these circles about four times.

It worked and Bailey walked slowly towards me. He stopped when he was an arm's length away. Again I repeated the circle until he came closer. Turning my back to him, I sent out a calming thought. I pictured our valley in my mind and hoped he would pick up on it.

I clinched the deal by slowly lifting out the pre-prepared sliced carrots from my pocket and, stretching my arm behind me, offered it to him. I waited a few seconds and then felt his muzzle gently take the offering. Carrots are not part of the equine language but I was trying to explain to him that if he stayed close I would feed him. And stay close he did.

I gestured to Marina for everyone to move out of the paddock. Bailey and I circled closer and closer to the bucket of food she'd prepared. I gently felt in my pocket for the ever-present bailing twine. Breathing deeply, I cleared my mind by singing, "you are my lucky star".

I circled again right up to the bucket and as he bent his head down, I slowly placed the twine over his neck. Marina approached him with a head collar and lead rope. Bailey was calm now and allowed the vet to do a quick assessment of his condition.

"His eye needs antibiotics."

"Okay. Can you check his heart and lungs please?"

"No, but I can do it tomorrow and bring the drops for his eyes."

"That's good. Let's stable him now and if you say he's not going to drop dead in a day or two, I'll arrange to transport him to my farm."

I glanced over at Eileen who had moved along the paddock rail and was puffing away on another cigarette, eyes wide open. She had never seen her friend in this guise. I was, to her, the idiot blonde with a nervous laugh who tripped over a lot.

We all exchanged mobile numbers, but before we left I whispered into Bailey's ear, "All will be well".

Driving back to Olvera, Eileen was unusually quiet for the first fifteen minutes.

"Are you okay, Eileen?"

"Gob-smacked Diane. How did you do that?"

"What? Do you mean Bailey? It was just horse-talk. Much easier then Spanish."

"But Diane, he's practically dead. He has no weight. How are you going to fix him?"

"That's no problem. I know a professional, Kate Hayes. She

lives in Spain and can fatten up anything. Kate will sort him out for me."

"Right. But how are you going to get him back to your place?"

We thought for a moment and both said, at the same time, "Andy and Julie".

I made the call and explained the problem. The magical words floated back to me through the phone, "No problem, I'll sort it."

All I now needed was Marina's 'go ahead' that Bailey was fit to travel.

Chinni makes her way down the hill and is now on the track, waiting for me to give her the command to take the girls home for supper. I look down at the valley and there is Hardy, keeping to Beau's timetable, crossing the river and eating the lush food on the sides of the banks.

He looks so out of place in this Andalucian valley and yet, quite at home, just like me. The 'golden moment' comes and envelopes the big old cob. He doesn't know it yet but tomorrow he will have a companion. Marina has called to say that Bailey is fit to travel. No more lonely nights.

The goats are now gathered around me. Patty, Alice and her daughters, are the last to come down off the hill. I lock eyes with Chinni. She has made this day her finest. Who knew what the future held for this brave, strong, kind girl?

I am so proud of her and silently, as we hold each other's gaze, I thank her. She waits for my last words of the day. I turn around to look at my goats.

We did it. We'd made it, and now it was time for supper.

"Are we ready, girls?" I ask, before turning to my friend.

"Take them home, Chinni, take them home."

So, what happened next?

Autumn in Andalucia is welcomed with open arms. The relentless heat of a Spanish summer takes its toll on goatherders and their animals. A gentle breeze in the afternoons allowed me and my friend and neighbour, Antonio, to walk our goats high in the hills in search of fresh grazing.

It also allowed us to sit and eat a late lunch without being attacked by a billion flies or my dear friend, Alice, the most cantankerous goat in the herd. Alice had sniffed out a carob tree and set off at high speed to devour as many pods before the rest of the herd caught up.

Antonio and I sat down at the very top of the hill and ate in companionable silence. The previous two hours had been spent arguing over which goat would be the first to give birth in late November. Two hundred goats were pregnant and during the next few months we needed to ensure the girls had the best food on offer.

We relax when we can because birthing time means little sleep and having to eat on the run. In the distance we can see the town of Olvera, its church and castle standing guard over the surrounding white-washed houses. I tried to spear a sardine from its small tin with my pocketknife when the church bells chimed dolefully. A funeral was in progress.

"That's old Pedro," said Antonio, scooping his sardine with a professionalism that left me in awe.

"Oh, how sad. Was he old?" I gave up on my knife, yanking the sardine out with my fingers.

"The clue, Lady Dee, is in his name." He handed me a piece of bread to help with my on-going sardine problem.

We sat in silence, listening to the melancholic bells, then Antonio broke into a rant.

"It's a big con."

"What's a con?" I mentally braced myself.

"Well, Pedro was about ninety years old, right?"

"Errr, right."

In fact I knew nothing about the poor old chap or where this rant was going. I prayed I could keep up.

"Right. So all his friends are about the same age."

He stared at me, waiting for a response.

"Well, yes, I expect they are, those that are still alive."

"Exactly. So they all have to walk up the steep hill to the church behind the hearse." He paused for dramatic effect, taking a puff from his roll-up. "Now do you see the scam?"

"No, I don't see. What are you talking about?"

"Old people walking up a steep hill before walking back down again. That's the con."

He began to shake his head, not understanding why I couldn't keep up with his train of thought.

"The undertakers are rubbing their hands with glee and sizing up their next client. Why not hire a bus so that the oldies can ride up to the church? No, that is not profitable. Make them walk and money in the bank is guaranteed!"

I looked around to make sure the herd was still close by before pondering over Antonio's theory. I had to admit, he was probably onto something. Now it was my turn to mess with his brain.

"So, Antonio, just for argument's sake, let's say you believe in reincarnation. What animal would you come back as? Would it be a goat?"

"Me? A goat? No, no. I will come back as an imperial eagle. What about you?"

"That's easy. I'll come back as my sister's cat. Central heating, lovely food, soft beds, it would be like heaven."

"A cat? A cat? You would come back as a CAT?"

"My sister's cat. Only my sister's cat. But for heaven's sake, Antonio, you want to be an eagle but you won't even go on a plane! Where is the logic?"

That quizzical stare came back at me again. The look I had become so accustomed to. The look that said: you are a complete idiot.

"Because, Diane, I would actually be an eagle."

A Request

Did you enjoy Butting Heads in Spain? If so, Diane would be ever grateful if you could hop over to Amazon, Goodreads or wherever you bought this book and scribble a review. It doesn't need to be long and you can rest assured, Diane reads and appreciates every one.

Amazon Link: https://bit.ly/LadyGoatherd1

About the Author

Diane Elliott was born in Kent but spent her adult life in Dorset. Although trained as a secretary, her dream was to work with horses. As an eight-year-old, she won many rosettes in horse competitions, particularly for the egg-and-spoon and musical sack races. Upon reflection, that was a good start for a budding goatherder.

Email: dianeelliott20@gmail.com
Photo Gallery: https://antpress.org/lady-goatherder-gallery/
Facebook Timeline: https://www.facebook.com/diane.eliott
Facebook Page: https://www.facebook.com/ExperienceOlvera

If you'd like to chat with Diane Elliott and other memoir authors and readers, do join We Love Memoirs. It's the friendliest group on Facebook.

https://www.facebook.com/groups/welovememoirs/

Acknowledgements

Grateful thanks to the following people:

Anne Marie and Zoe of Olvera Properties. Ian and Laurie, Julie, Andy and Anne. Nital Nagel, Alyson Atkinson and Sue Lightly for their support and friendship. All the wonderful friends who sponsored a goat. Alan and Lorna who have been our inspiration.

My wonderful family, Pete, Amelia, Felicity, Sandra, Hazel who kept the faith and our spirits high.

Thanks to Pat Ellis, Julie Haigh, Elizabeth Moore and Beth Haslam for reading advance copies of this book and for their valuable suggestions.

Finally, thanks and gratitude to my friend and publisher, Victoria Twead, and Ant Press for all their work. Thanks not only for their professional services but hand-holding throughout the process and their attention to detail. Thanks to Mikki Rowland for the wonderful painting of Alice on the cover. You captured her perfectly.

Diane Elliott, January 2022.

Ant Press Books

AWESOME AUTHORS ~ AWESOME BOOKS

If you enjoyed this book, you may also enjoy these Ant Press titles:

MEMOIRS

Dear Fran, Love Dulcie: Life and Death in the Hills and Hollows of Bygone Australia collated by Victoria Twead

Butting Heads in Spain: Lady Goatherder 1 by Diane Elliott

Chickens, Mules and Two Old Fools by Victoria Twead (Wall Street Journal Top 10 bestseller)
Two Old Fools ~ Olé! by Victoria Twead
Two Old Fools on a Camel by Victoria Twead (thrice New York Times bestseller)
Two Old Fools in Spain Again by Victoria Twead
Two Old Fools in Turmoil by Victoria Twead
Two Old Fools Down Under by Victoria Twead
One Young Fool in Dorset (Prequel) by Victoria Twead
One Young Fool in South Africa (Prequel) by Joe and Victoria Twead
Two Old Fools Boxset, Books 1-3 by Victoria Twead

Fat Dogs and French Estates ~ Part I by Beth Haslam
Fat Dogs and French Estates ~ Part II by Beth Haslam
Fat Dogs and French Estates ~ Part III by Beth Haslam
Fat Dogs and French Estates ~ Part IV by Beth Haslam

Fat Dogs and French Estates ~ Part V by Beth Haslam
Fat Dogs and French Estates ~ Boxset, Parts 1-3 by Beth Haslam

From Moulin Rouge to Gaudi's City by EJ Bauer
From Gaudi's City to Granada's Red Palace by EJ Bauer

South to Barcelona: A New Life in Spain by Vernon Lacey

Heartprints of Africa: A Family's Story of Faith, Love, Adventure, and Turmoil by Cinda Adams Brooks
How not to be a Soldier: My Antics in the British Army by Lorna McCann
Moment of Surrender: My Journey Through Prescription Drug Addiction to Hope and Renewal by Pj Laube

One of its Legs are Both the Same by Mike Cavanagh
A Pocket Full of Days, Part 1 by Mike Cavanagh
A Pocket Full of Days, Part 2 by Mike Cavanagh

Horizon Fever 1: Explorer A E Filby's own account of his extraordinary expedition through Africa, 1931-1935 by A E Filby
Horizon Fever 2: Explorer AE Filby's own account of his extraordinary Australasian Adventures, 1921-1931 by A E Filby

Completely Cats - Stories with Cattitude by Beth Haslam and Zoe Marr

Fresh Eggs and Dog Beds: Living the Dream in Rural Ireland by Nick Albert
Fresh Eggs and Dog Beds 2: Still Living the Dream in Rural Ireland by Nick Albert
Fresh Eggs and Dog Beds 3: More Living the Dream in Rural Ireland by Nick Albert
Fresh Eggs and Dog Beds 4: More Living the Dream in Rural Ireland by Nick Albert

Don't Do It Like This: How NOT to move to Spain by Joe Cawley, Victoria Twead and Alan Parks

Longing for Africa: Journeys Inspired by the Life of Jane Goodall. Part One: Ethiopia by Annie Schrank
Longing for Africa: Journeys Inspired by the Life of Jane Goodall. Part Two: Kenya by Annie Schrank

A Kiss Behind the Castanets: My Love Affair with Spain by Jean Roberts
Life Beyond the Castanets: My Love Affair with Spain by Jean Roberts

The Sunny Side of the Alps: From Scotland to Slovenia on a Shoestring by Roy Clark

FICTION

A is for Abigail by Victoria Twead (Sixpenny Cross 1)
B is for Bella by Victoria Twead (Sixpenny Cross 2)
C is for the Captain by Victoria Twead (Sixpenny Cross 3)
D is for Dexter by Victoria Twead
The Sixpenny Cross Collection, Vols 1-3 by Victoria Twead

NON FICTION

How to Write a Bestselling Memoir by Victoria Twead
Two Old Fools in the Kitchen, Part 1 by Victoria Twead

LARGE PRINT BOOKS

Chickens, Mules and Two Old Fools by Victoria Twead (Wall Street Journal Top 10 bestseller)
Two Old Fools ~ Olé! by Victoria Twead
Two Old Fools on a Camel by Victoria Twead (thrice New York Times bestseller)
Two Old Fools in Spain Again by Victoria Twead
Two Old Fools in Turmoil by Victoria Twead
Two Old Fools Down Under by Victoria Twead
One Young Fool in Dorset (The Prequel) by Victoria Twead

One Young Fool in South Africa (The Prequel) by Joe and Victoria Twead

Fat Dogs and French Estates ~ Part I by Beth Haslam
Fat Dogs and French Estates ~ Part II by Beth Haslam
Fat Dogs and French Estates ~ Part III by Beth Haslam
Fat Dogs and French Estates ~ Part IV by Beth Haslam
Fat Dogs and French Estates ~ Part V by Beth Haslam

A Kiss Behind the Castanets: My Love Affair with Spain by Jean Roberts

Horizon Fever 1: Explorer A E Filby's own account of his extraordinary expedition through Africa, 1931-1935 by A E Filby
Horizon Fever 2: Explorer AE Filby's own account of his extraordinary Australasian Adventures, 1921-1931 by A E Filby

A is for Abigail by Victoria Twead (Sixpenny Cross 1)
B is for Bella by Victoria Twead (Sixpenny Cross 2)
C is for the Captain by Victoria Twead (Sixpenny Cross 3)

How to Write a Bestselling Memoir by Victoria Twead

CPSIA information can be obtained
at www.ICGtesting.com
Printed in the USA
LVHW081747210122
708924LV00012B/1326

9 781922 476562